HOW TO TALK GOLF

HOW TO TALK GOLF

by Dawson Taylor

Illustrated by Taylor Jones

Robson Books

This edition first published in Great Britain in 2000 by Robson Books, 10 Blenheim Court, Brewery Road, London N7 9NT

A member of the Chrysalis Group plc

First published by Robson Books as *Golf: The Essential Companion* First published in the USA by Barricade Books Inc, 150 Fifth Avenue, Suite 700, New York, NY 10011

British Library Cataloguing in Publication Data
A catalogue record for this title is available from the British Library

ISBN 1 86105 312 6

Printed by WS Bookwell, Finland

CONTENTS

INTRODUCTION

Where did anyone ever get the idea of striking a little ball a number of times with ridiculous looking implements so as to drive it great distances and then putting it into a little round hole only 4¼ inches in diameter? Where did it all start? How long ago?

'Way back in the 1600s in Holland, the Dutch played a game called "Het Kolven." There are contemporary paintings and literature which tell us that the game was played in wide open spaces such as on frozen lakes or rivers, or roads and that a ball was struck from a tee and flew long distances in the air from one stake or marker to another similar stake or marker. We also know that the ball had to be played from the exact spot where it happened to come to rest on the ground or ice.

The clubs used then were startlingly like the wooden shafted golf clubs of the late 1800s. They were slender wooden instruments with leather grips and graceful heads of metal or wood that were attached to a supple shaft by "whipping" or wrapping with closely laid cord or line. The ball then in use was small and light but there is no doubt that it flew long distances when struck properly. We assume that in the 1600s the Dutch were playing a game closely related to the game of golf as we know it today.

The earliest reference to golf in Scotland occurs as early as 1457 in a decree by King James II that "anyone who wasted his time at futball and the golf should be punished."

In 1776 the links of St. Andrews, Scotland were being used for golf and one William Gib was given permission to use the links for the raising of rabbits but the links were "not to be spoiled where the golfing is used." The rabbits multiplied, as rabbits are apt to do. In a few years the golfers of St. Andrews were permitted a "free drop" from any rabbit burrow that entrapped their golf balls. That is, they could pick the ball up and move it away from the trouble, and strike it from a fairer lie.

In 1754 the rules of golf were formally introduced by golfers who called themselves the Royal and Ancient Golf Club, Royal because one of their members was the King of England himself. Their rules, with surprisingly few modifications, continue to govern the game of golf today no matter where it is played all over the world. There is one simple rule in golf—you take your club (you have quite a selection of clubs with faces of various "lofts") and attempt to strike a round rubber or super-polymer golf ball (1.68 inches in diameter and weighing 1.68 ounces) from here to there in the least number of strokes. The "there" is represented by a hole in the ground 4¼ inches in diameter.

Over the centuries the language of golf has evolved in much the same way as the game itself came to be refined into beautifully-kept garden-type golf courses ranging from 6,000 to 7,000 yards with 18 individual holes which the golfer is expected to play "from tee to green", the tee being the starting spot and the green the closely cropped area where the hole is.

The language is colorful and descriptive. A "whiff" or complete miss of the ball is certainly a word that comes from the sound of the act itself. A "dub" is probably another one for the golfer who is a dub, a weak player who hits the ball with a sound like "dub."

Over the several hundred years of golf history many unusual terms and expressions have found their way into the language of golf. Some of them, such as the word "dormie" (which describes the situation where one player is so far ahead of another he cannot lose) is so old that no one really knows its origin.

The game of golf was brought to this continent in the early 1870s. The Royal Montreal Golf Club was formed then by Scots who had come over to the New World and brought with them their baffies and gutties and their knowledge of how to lay out a demanding golf course on rolling hills and dales.

In 1884 Russell Montague, a New Englander who had studied law in London, came to the White Sulphur Springs area in West Virginia.

He had played golf in Scotland and loved the game. He laid out a ru-
dimentary 6-hole course at Oakhurst, West Virginia and with a few
friends began the first true golf club in the United States where regular tournaments were played and silver medals awarded to the lowest
scorer.

From the 1890s on interest in the new game grew rapidly. At first
it was a social game meant primarily for the rich. Golf balls were expensive and the common man could not afford to play the game. In
1898 Coburn Haskell had the brilliant idea of making a golf ball by
winding rubber-bands around a core. The result was the Haskell ball
which replaced the hard "billiard-ball" gutta percha which had been
in general use for a number of years.

With the invention of the rubber-wound Haskell ball the cost of
golf balls was reduced drastically and many more players could afford the game.

In the early 1900s Harry Vardon, a great English golf champion,
visited the States and played a number of exhibition golf matches.
His slashing style, his accuracy, his long-driving ability caught the
fancy of the Americans. Golf took off in America.

In the 1920s the most charismatic golfer of all time appeared in
the person of Robert T. Jones, Jr. A soft-spoken Southerner, he was
a boy wonder of golf and by the time he retired from golf competition at the age of 28 he had set records that would never again be
equaled. Furthermore he had captured the hearts of America with
his charming personality. When he returned from Scotland after winning both the British Open and Amateur Championships he was
greeted by a tremendous ticker-tape welcome in New York with several million people shouting their acclaim for his accomplishments.

"Bobby" Jones, Walter Hagen and Gene Sarazen dominated the
golf scene in the 1920s and then came the era of Ben Hogan, Byron
Nelson and Sam Snead. The 1960s saw the rise of Arnold Palmer,
Gary Player, Billy Casper and Gene Littler. Lurking in the wings was
a stout, stocky young man from Ohio. In 1959 and 1961 he had won
the U.S. Amateur Championships. He said he was not interested in
playing professional golf but when he changed his mind and turned

professional in 1961 Jack Nicklaus came to dominate golf as it had never been done before. Not long afterward another marvelous golfer, Tom Watson, came on the scene to challenge the King and as the 1980s march on we have seen an invasion of great foreign players in the persons of Severiano Ballesteros of Spain, Bernhard Langer of Germany and Isao Aoki of Japan, among others.

Early on all men golfers wore knickers. The roughs were deep then and oftentimes were brambly. Long trousers with cuffs could get in the way of a golfer deep in the "jungle." Knickers did not.

Golfers then wore shoes with smooth rubber soles or else wore shoes with rubber cleats, not unlike those on the shoes football players wear today. The teeing area was frequently a bare twelve-by-twelve-inch square of hard-packed grassless ground. There, the golfer teed his ball upon a conical mound of sand. At every tee there was a tee-box full of sand with a bucket of water suspended above it. It was the caddie's duty to wash the player's ball using the sand to scrub it and then to make the tee for his player. He did this by pouring some of the water onto the sand, and then, with a gob of wet sand in his hand he would form a miniature volcano-like structure on the hard ground and tee his player's ball on the top of it. He had to know his player's preference, too, as to tee height to insure a good tip after the round was over.

In the 1920s a wooden tee, the Reddy Tee, was invented. The teeing ground became softer with short cut grass on ground that would accept a wooden tee. Tee-boxes then gradually disappeared, never to be seen again.

In the early 1900s a serviceable set of nine wooden-shafted clubs could be bought for the equivalent of $75.00 today. The average golfer carried a driver, a brassie (named for the brass plate on its bottom), and a spoon with greater face loft than the brassie. Iron clubs were wooden-shafted of hickory—a midiron, mid-mashie, mashie, mashie-niblick, niblick and a putter, the counterparts of today's 2-iron, 4-iron, 5-iron, 7-iron, and 9-iron. A set of clubs like this was not heavy so most golfers carried their own clubs in what were called "Sunday" or "Pencil bags" with a diameter of eight to ten inches.

Not until the days of Jones in the late 1920s and early 1930s was

there any thought of matching clubs in weight and flexibility. Bobby
Jones is credited with having one of the first sets in which the clubs were closely matched to each other.

Golf club manufacturers produced matched sets of clubs with irons from 1 to 11. Walter Hagen once used a set with twenty-four clubs, numbered 1, 1½, 2, 2½, 3, 3½ and so on. The Spalding company had made a deal with Bobby Jones to manufacture clubs with his imprint. They were so fearful that the golfers of that day would not accept the shiny appearance of the steel-shafted club that they colored them yellow to simulate the look of the hickory shafts. But the chromium plated shaft was accepted and is the standard of today.

Then the United States Golf Association, the ruling body of American golf, stepped in and decided that the golfer would be allowed to carry no more than fourteen clubs in regulation play. The USGA also began to study the effect of different materials and compressions in golf balls. Golfers were driving "hot" golf balls prodigious distances. Courses which had bunkers designed to trap the player's ordinary drive were being by-passed as the ball flew over them more frequently than not. The USGA in cooperation with some of the golf club and golf ball manufacturers developed a mechanical golf driving machine dubbed "Iron Byron" because it seemed to duplicate the wonderful swing of great golfer Byron Nelson.

Thousands of hours of testing of balls and equipment brought standardization in equipment and rules governing the initial velocity of the golf ball. Today no golf ball is allowed in play with an initial velocity of more than 255 feet per second.

Most of the professional golfers of early days came from the ranks of the caddies. Few of them were college-educated. Nowadays most of the good golfers of the United States, both men and women, come from Junior Golf programs and from intensive college golf programs that grant scholarships to likely golf prospects. Golf is now recognized as a serious college competitive sport. College golf matches act as great training grounds for the golfers of today and tomorrow. But players who want to gain admission to the PGA tour still must obtain their playing cards by successfully completing a qualifying school course.

Prize money in the early days of golf was scandalously low. In the early U.S. Open Tournaments the winner was awarded a medal. In 1931 the USGA awarded Billy Burke, the winner, a prize of $1,000. Twenty-first place that year brought Olin Dutra $25.00. It was not until 1947, when Lew Worsham beat Sam Snead at St. Louis Country Club, that first prize money was increased to $2,000. That year thirty-first place paid $75.00. As late as 1946 the prize for the winner of the British Open Championship was £150, worth $600 at that time. Sam Snead won it that year and gave the entire sum to his caddie. In 1984 Severiano Ballesteros' purse for winning the British Open was £55,000, about $70,000 in American money.

Today golf purses have grown astronomically large. Recently, in an unofficial golf match TV audiences watched Jack Nicklaus win a quarter of a million dollars in a "Skins" game, a kind of winner-takes-all format.

Here are some unusual facts about the way purses have improved over the years in both mens' and ladies' professional golf.

In 1948 Mildred "Babe" Zaharias was the leading money winner with $3,400. In 1984 Betsy King won $266,771.

In 1941 Ben Hogan was the leading money winner with $18,358. In 1984 Tom Watson won $476,260.

In 1965 the U.S. Walker Cup team defeated the team of Great Britain-Ireland. On the U.S. team were six young players who soon turned pro—Gary Koch, Curtis Strange, Jerry Pate, George Burns, Craig Stadler and Jay Haas. As of the end of 1984 these six golfers had won prize money totalling nearly $7,000,000.

How high is the prize money going? Million dollar purses have been put up but so far no golfer has won one because they usually involve the winning of two or three designated tournaments in one year.

But while golf fans would like to see this happen, true afficionados would rather make successive pars or birdies or fire an ace.

LEXICON

Ace

n: a single shot from the tee ending up in the cup. Also known as a hole-in-one. If the ball comes to rest against the flagstick, the flagstick may be removed (gently) so as to allow the ball to fall to the bottom of the cup. Billy Joe Patton scored an ace in that manner on the 6th hole of the Augusta National course in the 1954 Masters.

address

v: to take one's stance and adjust the club preparatory to hitting the ball.

air shot

n: a whiff, a complete miss of the ball. One of the most embarrassing shots in golf at any time, but especially so on a first tee with an audience looking on.

Gary Player

alternate stroke

n: a variation of the game of golf in which two partners take turns in striking the ball. A very old golf game, it still is played in modern times in International Ryder Cup (Professional), Walker, and Curtis Cup (Amateur) matches as well as at many golf clubs that uphold the traditions of golf.

TEE HEE HEE

amateur golfer

n: one who plays the game for pleasure rather than for financial benefit or professional reasons.

away

n: after the initial shots off the tee, the expression used to designate the golfer farthest from the hole who always plays first. He is said to be "away." This is true even if one player's ball is on the green and the other's is in a bunker. It is also said to have been Ben Hogan's favorite expression. Jimmy Demaret, who played with Ben a great deal, was asked if Ben ever spoke to him during a round. Jimmy said, "Sure, on every hole when we reached the green he'd say, "You're away."

Ben Hogan

Back nine

n: the second nine of an 18~hole golf course. On many early golf courses the first nine holes were laid straight out from the clubhouse and then the golfer turned and came back "in." See "turn" and "in."

backspin

n: the reverse spin imparted to the ball as the grooved club strikes down on it at impact. The depth of face grooves is governed by the Rules of Golf. In the early days deeper grooves were allowed and the result was that a good golfer could do tricks with backspin and side spin (imparted by a "cut" shot).

baffy

n: a wooden club of the early days of golf with greater loft than a spoon (3~wood). It would be considered in the 4~ or 5~wood range in today's game.

Bakspin mashie

n: a wooden~shafted club with 5~iron loft and deeply grooved face. The club was declared illegal in the 1920s, but as it could make the ball do wondrous things golfers gave it up reluctantly.

banana ball

n: a slice, that is, a ball that curves quickly to the right for a right~handed golfer or to the left for a left~handed golfer, as a result of an outside to inside swing that causes the ball to rotate counter~clockwise.

best ball

n: the selection of the lowest sin~ gle score of a foursome on a hole as the score of the entire four~ some for that hole. In foursome competition it is a favor~ ite game of American players who have high handicaps that bring their scores down close to those of the bet~ ter players. Example: Players A, B, and C have 5s while player D has a 4. The "best ball" is the 4.

better ball

n: the selection of the lower of two scores on a hole as the score of a twosome for that hole. "Better ball" is always used in twosome play, "best ball" in foursome play.

between the markers

prep. phrase: the teeing ground is always designated by two markers placed on a line perpendicular to the line of play. The golfer may tee up directly on the line between the markers or anywhere in the rectangle made by two club-lengths on a line straight back of each marker. If he plays his ball from in front of the marker, he may not count the stroke, must re~tee it properly, and is charged a penalty stroke for the error.

birdie

n: a score one less than par on a hole. Also called a "bird." Note: You don't "make a birdie" today, you "make bird," or you are not "cool."

Chi Chi Rodriguez

bisque

n: a handicap stroke given by one player to another. The player getting the stroke may apply it to any hole he wishes, but must notify his opponent in advance of playing that hole that he is "taking his bisque." (Pronounced bisk).

bite

n: "bite" results on a well~struck iron shot when the

blade of the club strikes the ball on the downswing and causes the ball to rotate with backspin, that is, from the bottom of the ball backward toward the top. When such a ball hits the green it bites. Usually the momentum of the ball will cause it to travel forward for a first hop and then the backspin bites and pulls it back.

Billy Casper

blade one

v: to hit the ball across its center line with the bottom edge of an iron club. The result is a ball that rockets off the club like a line drive in baseball.

blade putter

n: a straight-faced metal putter, sometimes with a small flange at the bottom, but always with a square top edge no more than a half-inch in width.

JoAnne Carner

blast

n: a forceful shot in a sand bunker or sometimes in a muddy ditch when a great deal of sand or mud is exploded with the shot. See "explosion shot." The heavy sand-wedge enters the surface of the bunker from one-and-one-half to two inches behind the ball, goes down under it, and ball and sand or mud blast out.

bogey

n: a score of one over par on a hole. In the early 1900s a British golfer one over par, mindful of Colonel Bogey in the marching song, "Colonel Bogey March," popular at that time said, "Even Colonel Bogey could have done better than that!" The name stuck from that time on. Playing "bogey golf" means playing at a one over par pace per hole, 45~45=90 on a 36~36=72 par course.

borrow

v: to aim the ball when on a sloping green a distance to the right or left of the cup depending upon the slope, so as to compensate for the amount of slope, and putt on the proper line to the cup. The amount taken in feet or inches is the "borrow." "I had to borrow six inches to get in on the high side of the cup."

brassie

n: a fairway wood with more loft than a driver but less than a spoon or 3~wood — designated a 2~wood today. Early brassies got their names from the fact that the sole~plate was made of brass.

brother~ in law act

Bruce Lietzke and Jerry Pate, brothers~ in~law for real.

n: an expression used to denote excellent meshing of scores by two partners in a two~ball event. An example: A birdie by partner A followed by a birdie by partner B and then another birdie by part~ner A. Sometimes you will hear the losers moan, "They brother~in~lawed us to death."

bull's~eye putter

n: a brass blade putter with an unusual curved~up heel. It is nearly center~shafted, giving it excellent balance. With the success of the original model some flanges have now been added. Developed about forty years ago by the Acushnet Company, it became one of the most popular putters of all time.

bunker

n: any obstacle, as a sand trap or grassy depression, constituting a hazard. The golfer is not permitted to rest the sole of his club on the ground or sand of a hazard as he prepares to play. Bun~kers vary greatly in size, shape, and depth. Hell Bunker at St. Andrews is about 50 yards wide, 25 yards long, and 15 feet deep. On the other hand, the tiny "Devil's ass~hole" bunker at Pine Valley in the United States is more like a pit 6 yards deep and sloping at the bottom like a funnel.

buried lie

n: the unfortunate situation that occurs when a ball hits soft turf or sand and practically burrows down out of sight. If it is truly out of sight the golfer is permitted to uncover the top of the ball so as to identify it as

(buried lie cont'd)

his own. A moderately buried lie in a sandtrap is called a "fried egg" in the United States because that's just what it looks like.

buttonhook

n: a putted ball that hits the cup on one side, goes around the back of it, rolling on the edge and shoots back out from the front edge of the cup toward the golfer. Bobby Jones once said, "When I saw my putt buttonhook, I knew I had lost the match."

Bobby Jones

Calamity Jane

n: the name Bobby Jones gave to his favorite wooden-shafted blade putter made for him by famous Scottish club-maker, Tom Stewart. Later in Jones' career a duplicate of the original was made for him when it was discovered that the center of Calamity Jane #1 had worn down from so many perfect putts on the face of the club. Jack Nicklaus recently had a number of duplicates of Calamity Jane made for some of his friends.

carried the hazard

v: the successful negotiation of a shot over a water hazard or a bunker. Also heard as "flew the bunker" which means the golfer successfully drove over it.

cash-in putter

n: a blade putter first manufactured by the Wright &

Ditson Company in the 1930s, then by Spalding. Several professionals on the tour today, notably Johnny Miller and Andy Bean, use the extremely popular cash~in putters.

casual water

Tom Watson

n: rain water in a fairway or rough. If the ball lies in casual water, the golfer may lift it and drop it without penalty in a dry place (if he can find one) nearby, but not nearer the hole. The rule is that if the golfer can see visible water under his shoes, he may declare the area cas~ual water. On the green, when casual water lies between the golfer's ball and the hole he may lift the ball and circle around, keeping the same distance to the hole, and attempt to find a dry path.

Chapman system

n: a method of partner play after the drive off the tee in which golfer #1 hits golfer #2's drive and vice versa. Then a choice is made as to which ball will be used for the final alternate stroke to the hole.

Lee Trevino

chili dip

n: a faulty "dipping" stroke on a short chip in which the club hits the ground first and then the ball. The result is usually a bad one with the ball moving only a few inches or feet.

chip~and~run

n: a shot played with a club that has a low loft such as a 4~iron or 5~iron that carries the ball over fringe or rough ground around a green and then allows the ball to run the rest of the way toward the cup. The ratio is usually one~third chip to two~thirds run.

chip shot

n: a delicate shot around the edge of a green usually made with a club of 4~iron, 5~iron, or 6~iron loft and intended to carry in the air and on the green and roll toward the hole.

cleek

n: a wooden~shafted club in the 4~iron or 5~iron range. Used for chip~and~run shots.

club

n: the implement used by the golfer to strike the ball. Has a head, a hosel, that connects a shaft to the head, and a grip of leather or a combination of rubber and cork. Today, a golfer is permitted to carry no more than 14 clubs in his bag. Walter Hagen played in the days before the 14 club rule went into effect. He used a set with 26 in all. He rewarded his caddie handsomely for carrying that monstrous load.

v: many golfers rely on their caddies to advise them about choice of clubs. In fact, many caddies are better golfers than the weekend players whose

grip

shaft

ferrule

face

toe

hosel

heel

sole

(club cont'd)

bags they carry. When a caddie recommends a 5~iron or a 6~iron for a particular shot, he is "clubbing" the player. In the British Open of 1960 Arnold Palmer bogeyed the par~4 Road Hole, the 17th at St. Andrews, three times in a row after hitting 6~iron seconds. On the last day he had the same shot into the green. He asked caddie "Tip" Anderson to give him his 5~iron. Tip said, "You'll go over the green with it!" Arnie insisted on the 5~iron. He hit and ran the ball over the green onto the road. But he chipped up then within a foot of the hole and made his 4. Arnie said, "See there, Tip, you've been giving me the wrong club all week."

concede

vt: to assume that your opponent can make that very short putt to win the hole and therefore count the ball in the cup as if he had taken and made the shot. Example: A hits out of bounds on his drive on a par~3 hole. B puts his ball on the green a foot from the hole. A, who would be hitting his 3rd shot to the green on his second ball would have good reason to "concede" the hole. On the green, when an opponent's putt is close to the hole for a sure win, it is polite for the other player to concede it by knocking it away.

cuppy lie

n: a ball in a cup~like depression. Usually on bare ground in the rough between two hanks of rough grass. Frequently an "impossible lie." All the golfer can do is hack and hope.

cut

v: to slash the cover off the golf ball. Until the invention of the solid "cut~proof" ball, the outer cover of a golf ball was frequently cut by the sharp edge of an iron hitting it "in the middle." Golf balls with cuts in them became unplayable because they were out of round. Today only the professionals and good amateurs play the wound~rubber, Surlyn~covered golf ball which still may be cut by a poor stroke.

n: the "cut" is the score in a golf tournament at which the field is narrowed after two days of play (three in the British Open). Usually the low forty (sometimes as many as sixty) players including ties make the cut and play the last two days.

cut shot

n: a shot played with any iron from a 4 to a wedge. where the golfer takes his club outside his normal line on his backswing and returns it from outside to in so as to impart spin to the ball. The cut ball spins in a clockwise fashion, stops quickly on the green, and rolls to the right. A cut shot is a trick shot or a "top drawer" shot by a pro.

Doug Sanders

Dance floor

n: the green or fairway. A ball that lands safely on the cut grass is said to be "on the dance floor."

dawn patrol

n: early morning golfers are the dawn patrol. From the famous old movie "Dawn Patrol" with Richard Arlen where the fighter planes went off at 5:00 a.m. in fog.

defender

n: an interesting betting game for three players in which each golfer "defends" against the other two on every third hole. Example: A, the defender, has 4 against B's 5 and C's 5 on the first hole. A wins 2 points, having defended the hole. If A had had a 6, he would have lost the hole and B and C would have won a point apiece. On the next hole B defends against A and C, on the third hole C defends against A and B, and so on.

dogleg

n: a golf hole shaped like a dog's leg. In fact, in Scotland the term is dog's leg. The dogleg hole can bend either way.

Fala

dormie

n: when one player is as many holes "up" or ahead of the other player as there are holes left to play. Example: A is 3 up on B with 3 holes to play. B would have to win all three holes to tie. A is said to be dormie. The player "up" is dormie. It is not the other way around.

double~eagle

n: a score 3~under par on a hole. The most famous

Gene Sarazen

(double~eagle cont'd)

double~eagle, "The shot heard around the world," was made by Gene Sarazen on the Par~5 485~yard 15th hole at Augusta National in the 1935 Masters. It enabled him to catch Craig Wood and tie for the lead. Gene then won the championship in a playoff.

driver

n: the longest club in the bag, 42 to 44 inches long, with a face from one~and~three~quarter inches to two~and~one~quarter inches deep and shallow loft (9° to 11°) in order to enable the golfer to "drive" the ball low and far. In recent years driv~er heads have been constructed of metal which leads to the anomaly of the name "metal wood."

driving iron

n: a long shafted iron club with a heavy head and very little loft. In the early days of golf, in the 1800s, all the golf clubs were made with wooden heads. In the 1870s the Scots began to make clubheads out of forged steel and thus the "iron" was born. With it came the driving iron.

driving range

n: a location from which practice shots may be played.

drop

n: to place a new ball or reposition the one in play

when a golfer loses a ball, hits it into a hazard, or into an unplayable lie. The golfer must add a penalty stroke to his score. Then he is allowed to "drop" the ball nearby where he will have a chance to advance it. He holds the ball out at arm's length and makes his drop. Watch how the good players in televised golf make a drop and try to choose a good "lie" for the next shot. Sometimes they get fooled when the ball rolls into another bad lie.

Horton Smith

dual-purpose wedge

n: one that can be used on the fairway as well as in the sand.

dub

v: to mishit a shot and cause it to dribble along the ground.

n: the golfer who mishits a lot of shots.

duck hook

n: a shot in which the ball "ducks" to the left as soon as it is hit. Much more dreaded than a slice or banana ball. Ben Hogan once said, "I get nauseated every time I hook."

duffer

n: a poor golfer, also known as a dub.

duffer's delight

n: the easiest club in the bag to use is a 5~iron because it has a moderately short shaft and is of medium loft. Because it sometimes is the only club a duffer can use well, it has come to be known as "duffer's delight."

dunch shot

n: a short shot into crunchy sand that makes a sound like "dunch" as the club strikes. The shot has little or no follow through.

dying putt

n: a putt that just barely reaches the cup and then falls in or stops very close to the hole. On very fast greens it is sometimes necessary to use this style of putt so that the ball will not run by the cup and result in a three~putt coming back.

Eagle

n: a score of two strokes under par on a hole.

Ray Floyd

explosion shot

n: a blast out of a sand bunker. The shot has the appearance of an explosion because the sand flies out along with the ball.

Face grooves

n: grooves cut into the face of a club parallel to the sole to make it possible to put spin on the ball. In the early days of golf the faces of the iron clubs were smooth. Then, clubs were grooved, deeper and deeper until the 1930s when the Royal and Ancient decreed that face grooves can be no deeper than .035 inches.

Arnold Palmer

fade

n: a gentle, controlled slice, only a few yards from left to right. To be distinguished from a banana ball which is a great big slice out of control.

fairway

n: the closely cropped grass that lies between the tee and the green. The fairway is bordered by the "rough," grass which is cut longer, ranging from an inch-and-a-half to six inches or more.

fat

adj: hitting the turf behind the ball instead of the ball. A ball hit "fat" will have no spin and usually the golfer suffers a loss of expected distance on his shot.

feather

vt: to put a delicate fade on a shot into the green. The

shot floats to the left of the hole and then "sits down" as light as a feather, working its way toward the hole with left to right spin.

featherie ball

n: in the early days of golf, the 1800s, golf balls were made out of leather stuffed tightly with goose feathers and then sewn, not unlike the way a baseball is sewn in modern times. The ball maker would boil a pound of feathers until they were softened and then, using a special tool, would stuff the leather cover as tightly as possible through a small hole in its side. The featheries were expensive, so golf then was a rich man's game. The invention of the gutta-percha (see "gutty") helped to bring down the cost so that the average man could enjoy the game.

flub

vt: to strike the ball poorly and move it only a few feet. "He flubbed the ball trying to get it out of the deep rough."

fluffy lie

n: a ball sitting high in the grass with considerable room for the club to get "under" the ball. A dangerous lie in the rough because it is practically impossible to impart spin to a ball from a fluffy lie.

foozle

vt: to make a bungling stroke, a complete mess of a shot. For example: In trying to loft a shot over a bun~ker to top the ball or "hit the ball in the head" and dribble it into the bunker.

fore...

n: the warning cry to the golfers on the course ahead to let them know that they are in danger of being hit by a golf ball. The usual response is for the golfer ahead to cov~er his head and duck.

fore~caddie

n: a caddie who is sent on ahead to stand near the driving area to observe where the tee shots land. Fore~caddies are used in tournaments where the rough is deep. In this way the players' balls can be found readily thereby avoiding delays due to long hunts for the sometimes hard to find golf balls.

forward press

n: the body movement with the hands and arms or with the body (sometimes an inward kick of the right knee), which initiates the backswing. The movement starts the body slightly forward toward the ball and then there is a reverse movement which lets the club~head be backward away from the ball in a smooth motion.

four~ball

n: a match in which four golfers used all four scores to determine the winning and losing of holes. There are many variations of four~ball matches including the high and low scores of a pair being matched against those of the other pair, or "aggregate"—the low score plus the total of the two scores of a pair.

fried egg

n: a ball in sand, slightly buried, and with a ridge of sand all around it.

fringe

n: the short grass just off the closely cut surface of the green.

frog hair

n: same as fringe. An expression popularized by Jimmy Demaret on early TV golf commen~ tating.

Funston's rule

n: "Always expect your opponent to hole out on his next stroke and you will never be surprised." Attributed to Irv Funston, a Michigan Seniors Champion.

Gallery

n: the cluster of spectators around the green in a tournament.

Ginty

n: a modern day version of the cleverly de~signed wooden club (see "baffy") with a V~shaped sole plate to help the clubhead get through heavy rough.

Give, give?

vt: what your opponent asks when his ball and your ball lie equally close to the hole on the green. It means, "I'll concede your putt if you will concede mine." Used most frequently by weak putters who are afraid of short putts.

gooseneck putter

n: a putter whose head is offset to the right as a result of an "L~bend" in the shaft near the hosel.

go to school

v: learning about the speed or direction of a putt by carefully observing another player's putt on the same line to the cup.

grain

n: the direction in which the grass grows on a green. Some greens are very "grainy," which means that in~stead of the blades standing straight up they lie in one direction or another like hair on a person's head. Grain

(grain cont'd)

can help to move a putt several inches one way or the other as it travels toward the cup. Watch the pros inspect the inside of the cup before they putt. They're trying to determine which way the grain of the grass lies. They also look for the shine on the green. If they can see it, it tells them the grain grows with the shine and the putt will roll faster with it than against it.

Judy Rankin

Grand Slam

n: winning all four major championships in one year—the United States and British Opens, the United States Professional Golfers Association championship, and the Masters Tournament.

Jan Stephenson

graphite

n: a recently developed golf club shaft material of spun carbon, lighter than its counterpart in steel, but subject to greater torque. Used mainly by women golfers.

green

n: the closely cut grassy area that surrounds the flag-stick and hole.

greenie

n: a bet as to who will be the first player to get his

ball on the green. On par~3s the "greenie" usually is won by the golfer whose ball is closest to the flagstick after all the players have made their tee~shots.

green jacket

n: the coat awarded to the winner of the Masters Tournament.

Jack Nicklaus, winner of five Masters.

gutty

n: also "guttie." In the 1870s an idol of the Indian God Vishnu was shipped to England protected by a gummy substance called gutta~percha. An enterprising Scot rec~ ognized its possibilities as a material for golf balls. Those fashioned out of it were called gutties. They were hard, like billiard balls, and had a low trajectory and they were used for a number of years until the invention in the late 1890s of the Haskell rubber~wound ball.

Halve

v: to tie the score on a hole in a match. Both A and B, playing a head~to~head match, have 4s on a hole. "A has halved the hole with B." The word is pronounced as if it has no "l", "have."

ham~and~egging

n: same as the Brother~in~law act. Two partners alternately winning holes for their side.

handicap

n: an allowance of strokes intended to even competition between two golfers of unequal ability. Example: A's usual game is at even par~72. B's game is at 82. B's handicap would be calculated at 80% of the difference between par~72 and 82 or 8 shots. When A plays B he has to "give" B 8 strokes, that is, lower B's score by one stroke a hole on eight different holes. The holes where strokes are "given" are determined by the degree of difficulty of a golf course with the hardest hole usually designated as the "#1 stroke hole."

hand mashie

n: an illegal, cheating toss of the ball by hand. Years ago sand traps were often deep enough to obscure a player from the view of his opponent. Cheating golfers were known to pick up the ball in a trap, pretend to make a golf swing, and then release the ball at the same moment throwing it toward the hole. Now that bunkers are shallower, the shot is not seen much anymore. More often it is now a "foot mashie" that moves a ball out of a bad lie in the rough when the opponent is not watching.

Haskell

n: Coburn Haskell was the inventor of the wound~rubber golf ball in 1898. The invention revolutionized golf. It brought the cost of balls down so that everyone could afford to play the game.

hazard

n: a golf course obstacle whether a bunker of sand or grass or a water~ course (lake, pond, ditch). A golfer may not "ground" his club in a hazard. That is, he may not set it down on the sand, grass, or water behind the ball before he makes his stroke. If he does so, he suffers a penalty of one stroke.

hickories

Bobby Jones

n: the strong wood of the hick~ ory tree, used for many years for the shafts of golf clubs. The golfers of the early days found the shafts strong enough to withstand a hard blow at a golf ball and yet flexible enough to give the shot some whip or kick at impact. In the late 1920s the steel shaft replaced the hickory shaft. However, it is still seen in "classic" re~ productions of old putters such as the famous "Calamity Jane" of Bobby Jones.

high side

n: any cup not on level ground has a high side as well as a low side. Since gravity helps the ball to fall into the cup, it is desireable for a putt to approach the cup on the high side, so it will have a better chance of falling in — also known as the "Pro side" of the

(high side cont'd)
cup because professionals are always using it to their advantage. The low side of the cup is also known as the "wrong side," the "duffer's side," or the "amateur side."

hit it in the head

n: an expression meaning to top the ball, hit it above the middle.

hole~in~one club

n: a group of golfers at a golf club agree that each of them will contribute a dollar or two to the member of the group who scores the next hole~in~one.

hole~in~one contest

n: a contest among golfers, all driving from the same tee to the same cup, to see who can make a hole~in~one. Usually the winner is the golfer whose ball is closest to the cup. However, there have been instances of golf~ ers actually holing out in such contests. The odds against making a hole~in~one are approximately 44,000 to 1, depending, of course, upon the length of the hole.

honor

n: the right to drive first from the next tee goes to the golfer with the lowest score on the previous hole. On the first tee golfers usually toss a coin to determine honor. In club matches the golfer whose name is on the top of match schedule has the honor on the first tee.

hook

n: a ball hit with a right to left curve caused by counter~clockwise rotation of the ball. A smoth~ered hook is one that takes off to the left as soon as it leaves the club face. A normal hook occurs at the tail end of the flight of the golf ball. A hook adds distance to a drive, about 17 yards on a 200~yard drive hit straight with the same power.

horseshoes

n: a putting game between two players, each one putting two balls. Scored like the game of horseshoes with single points for the closest ball or balls and 3 points for an ace. The win~ner is the one who reaches a total of 21 first.

hosel

n: the hollow part of an iron club into which the shaft is fitted.

hot~dog pro

n: an "unknown" professional playing in a competition with other better known pros. The name originates from the dialogue, "Who's the pro coming up to the hole now? He's a nobody, let's go get a hot dog."

hunching

n: the illegal "stealing" one~half to one inch closer to the hole in replacing a ball marked on the green.

(hunching cont'd)

Under the rules the ball must be replaced exactly where it was when first marked. Cheaters try to take an illegal advantage and move the ball forward.

hustler

n: a con~man on the golf course who will hide his true ability in order to get favorable betting odds. Lee Trevino was an acknowledged hustler in his early days and one time pretended to be the locker~room boy at a golf club in order to "take" Raymond Floyd. Lee walked away with the money. Lee says that "A true hustler is one who can bet a hundred dollar Nassau without any money in his pocket.

Lee Trevino

Imaginary cup

n: coined by Horton Smith, one of the greatest putters of all time, the possessor of "The Velvet Touch." He said "all putts are level except sometimes the cup isn't where it's supposed to be." On a breaking putt, he would move the cup in his mind's eye to one side and putt straight for that imaginary cup allowing the break to carry the ball into the hole.

immaculate shot

n: a perfect shot, straight, and heading for the hole.

impossible lie

n: a lie from which the ball cannot be advanced

successfully. Occasionally a golfer finds his ball in such a terrible place that the shot is "impossible." Examples: lodged under the lip of a bunker, under a tree with the tree trunk obstruct~ ing the backswing, or a pitch to a severely sloping green with no chance to stop the ball near the cup.

impregnable quadrilateral

n: the name that Grantland Rice, sports writer, gave to the four major championships won by Bobby Jones in 1927, the United States and British Opens, the United States and British Amateur championships.

in

n: the second nine of a golf course, the "in nine." Early golf courses went "out" and then turned around and came "in."

Craig Stadler

in jail

prep. phrase: when a golfer's ball is in an impenetrable jungle, or behind a tree or trees directly on the line to the green, he is said to be in jail.

in your pocket

prep. phrase: when your ball lies with~ in a foot or two of the hole, it is said that "you have your birdie on par in your pocket."

in the leather

prep. phrase: originally "within the leather," the phrase denotes the boundary of "gimmie" putts in some friendly matches not played under the strict rules of golf that require all putts to be holed. The clubhead is put inside the hole on the side near the ball with the shaft on the ground pointed toward the ball. If the ball is within the length of the shaft, but does not reach the "leather" or bottom part of the grip, the putt is conceded. Hustlers have been known to shorten their putter grips so as to gain an extra inch of advantage when putts "in the leather" are given.

irons

n: golf clubs with either forged or cast iron heads. They range from the #1 iron to the #9 iron with lofts from nine or ten degrees for the #1 iron to as much as thirty-five degrees for the specialty clubs such as the pitching wedge or sand wedge. In the early days of golf the clubs had distinctive names which were lost when the steel shaft came into vogue in the late 1920s. The early names were mid-iron, mid-mashie, mashie, mashie-niblick, niblick, and putter.

Jigger

n: the old name used for a cleek, an iron club with 4-iron or 5-iron loft. Often used for chipping to the green.

Knee-knocker

n: a putt in the 2-to 4- foot range

which causes the golfer mental and physical problems. His knees "knock" in fear that he may miss the putt. It is also called a "white knuckler" because of tension in the fingers.

Lag

v: to putt cautiously so that the ball does not run by the cup if you miss the hole. This generally indicates that the golfer is attempting to get down in two putts for sure and does not worry if he misses his first putt.

lay off

v: a golfer "lays off" his golf club when he breaks his wrists improperly at the top of his back swing.

leader board

n: a large billboard type of display showing the current standing in relation to par of the leaders of a medal tournament. Originated at the Augusta National Golf Course for the Masters Tournament. Red and green numbers are used to show scores under or over par. A Red 3 means that the golfer is 3 under par, a Green 3 means that the golfer is 3 under par.

leave it

v: the order to "leave the flagstick in the hole" so the player can use it in making his shot. The golf ball cannot be on the putting surface when this order is given.

lift and clean

v: under wet conditions the ball often will embed itself or plug in the fairway and mud will adhere to it. When this happens, a "lift and clean" rule is put into effect by the Golf Committee. The player may pick up his ball, clean it, and return it close to its original spot.

links

n: sandy, undulating land built up along a coastline. Since early golf courses were built on links the name came to be designated the golf course itself, "golf links."

lip

n: the edge of the cup.

v: the act of rimming the cup, that is, the ball rolls around the edge, but does not fall into the cup.

loop

n: a peculiarity in the golf swing in which the golfer performs an exaggerated clockwise motion with his hands at the top of the swing to bring the club back to the ball on an inside track. Miller Barber, Hubert Green, and Gay Brewer are notable examples of good golfers with loops in their swings.

Gay Brewer

low side

n: when the cup is not on level ground, the one side lower than the other is called the low side. See "high side."

Make the cut

v: in tournament play the score among the low 40 or 60 players, depending upon the Committee's ruling as to the cut-off score — usually determined at the end of the second day of a 4-day medal tournament

mallet-head

n: a barrel-shaped head on a putter, flat on the striking surface and usually rounded at the rear.

marker

n: (1) an official scorer who not only records the player's score but also observes the play to see that the rules of golf are obeyed.

n: (2) a coin or similar object which is placed directly behind the ball so that its place can be "marked" when the ball is lifted. The stymie rule (see "stymie") is no longer played, so any ball on the putting green that may interfere with the line of another player's putt is lifted and marked at the request of that player.

Nancy Lopez

marshall

n: traffic directors for the gallery.

mashie niblick

n: the name in the early days of golf for an iron now in the 7-iron range.

Masters

n: the name assumed by the Augusta National Invitational Golf Tournament a few years after its first tournament in 1934. Because Robert T. Jones, Jr. wanted champions and other excellent players, the "masters of golf," to participate, the tournament came to be called the "Masters."

meat off my fork

n: when a player unexpectedly holes out a putt, a bunker shot or a chip to tie a hole he appeared to be losing, the player who has been tied will say, "You took the meat off my fork," meaning he expected to win the hole but either a good shot or fate ruled otherwise.

midget-killer

n: a drive that travels very low to the ground and never rises more than a foot or two in its flight.

mid-iron

n: in the early days of golf, the name for a 2-iron.

mid-mashie

n: old name for the 4-iron of today.

miss the cut

v: fail to qualify for the last two days of tournament play. See "cut."

mixed foursomes

n: play in which there are two foursomes, each con-sisting of a man and a woman.

move your mark

v: a request that a golfer move his marker out of the line of the requester's putt. The opponent will then lift the coin, measure one club head to the right or left of the line, but the same distance from the hole, and move the marker there. The reverse procedure is carried out when the ball is returned to its original marked spot.

muckle

adj: an old Scottish term for the broken down part of a cup. "He was always going in the muckle side of the cup.

Mulligan

n: a free second shot off the first tee if the first shot is bad. Fergus O'Shaughnessy Mulligan was a famous Irish golfer of the 1890s. He was Club Champion of Parknasilla links in County Kerry no less than fifteen times. But he had one peculiarity. If he had a poor drive from the first tee he would insist that he could call the round off and start over again with another ball. His opponents tolerated this peculiar custom and soon everyone claimed to be entitled to a "Mulligan" on the first tee. Even Ben Hogan has been known to take one once in a while. Sometimes players even allow

(Mulligan cont'd)

"choosies" which means that if the Mulligan shot is not as good as the first one, the golfer can elect to play his first instead. Incidentally, at Franklin Hills, a prominent Jewish club in Birmingham, Michigan a Mulligan is called a "Rosenberg."

Nassau

n: the name for a system for scoring or betting that originated in the Bahamas in the 1920s. Ryder Cup, Walker Cup and Curtis Cup matches are conducted at match play on a Nassau style of scoring. Three points are at stake. One point is awarded to the winner of each nine and one point for the overall match. Many golfers often make bets on a Nassau basis with one dollar riding on each point and in a few cases larger amounts.

never up, never in

n: an expression meaning unless you hit the ball at least as far as the hole, you will never hole it. Also stated as "never up, never down."

niblick

n: the old name for the 9~iron.

O.B.

n: stands for "out~of~bounds"——a ball that carries

beyond the boundary of the golf course. Costs the player one penalty stroke and he must play again from the spot where the unfortunate shot originated. The expression is believed to have been coined in Ireland in the 1930s at Ballybunion where there is a graveyard to the right of the first hole and Finbar O'Brien's farm beyond it. Many a tee~shot was either "in the graveyard" or "O.B."

one~iron

n: the straightest faced iron of all, meant to drive the ball far and low. Often used off the tee for greater accuracy. Therefore, it is also known as a "driving iron."

"The Open"

n: the name given to the open golf tournament held in the British Isles.

U.S. Open

n: the annual golf tournament conducted by the United States Golf Association. "Open" to all, amateurs as well as professionals. Actually, an amateur must have a handicap of 3 or better in order to attempt to qualify for the tournament.

out

n: the first nine holes of an 18~hole course constitute the "out nine."

outside agency

n: anything outside the golf course and not part of it that unfairly affects the golf ball by moving it. A dog, for instance.

Paddle grip

n: the name of the grip of a flat~sided putter in which in order to propel the ball toward the hole the flat~sided plane is at the same angle a ping~pong paddle would have.

par

n: the score an expert player would be expected to make on a given hole, allowing for two strokes on the putting green. Yardages for par per hole:

	Men	Women
Par~3	up to 250	up to 210
4	251 to 470	211 to 400
5	471 and over	401 to 575
6		576 and over

peg

n: the name first given to wooden tees. Until the invention of the wooden tee in the 1920s golfers used wet sand to form a conical mound from which they struck the tee~shot.

pick it up

v: what your opponent says when he concedes your putt.

pin

n: the flagstick.

ping

n: a currently famous and very popular putter which features a "cavity back" or hollow which spreads the effective power of the club over a wider face surface.

hosel

Der Bingle

pipe

n: another name for the hosel or neck of an iron. "He hit it on the pipe," means he shanked it.

pistol-grip

n: a putter grip with a curved handle at the top not unlike that of a pistol.

pitch

v: to loft the ball in the air to the green from a spot not very far from the green, usually in order to avoid a hazard or uneven ground between the ball and the green. "There are no bunkers in the air," is an old expression which explains why golfers like to pitch the ball rather than run it to the hole.

pitch-and-run

n: to be distinguished from the chip-and-run. In this shot the ball is pitched, or lofted from just off the green, in the air one-half to two-thirds of the way to the cup and then allowed to run to the hole. The different lofts of 8-iron, 9-iron, or wedge permit great variations in the results of the shot.

pitching wedge

n: a lofted club with a flange on the bottom specially designed for pitch shots from the fairway or rough.

playing the odd

n: the act of causing your opponent to play his shot after you have played yours. Bobby Jones was a master of this strategy and would intentionally play his tee~ shots short of his opponent's. Jones would hit his next shot close to the hole. The pressure was then on the opponent to match the shot.

play through

v: one group of golfers steps aside and allows the follow~ ing group to play the hole the first group was on — usually as a result of some delay such as an unsuccessful search for a lost ball. This is golf etiquette — the fact that slow players realize they may be holding up faster players — and allow them to play through as a matter of courtesy.

plugged lie

n: a ball embedded in its own divot~mark in the ground.

plumb bob

v: the act of sighting "through" a putter shaft suspended per~ pendicularly to the ground. By using one eye and closing the other some golfers can

(plumb bob cont'd)

determine the amount of slope from ball to hole.

practice tee

n: the separate practice area where golfers may use every club in the bag. A practice green and practice bunker often adjoin the practice tee.

press

v: to add another bet, basically a double or nothing bet, to the one that is in effect.

n: "I'll give you a press," means I will bet you the same amount as the original bet for the remaining holes. Example: A wins the 5th hole of a nine hole match and becomes 2 up with 4 holes to play. B presses him for the last 4 holes, thus making an equal but a separate bet for the remaining holes. If B can win the press bet he can offset a loss of the bet for the nine holes and come out even. Usually a press bet cannot be offered unless one player or the other is two holes ahead.

An "automatic press" is one that is agreed in advance and need not be further discussed between the players. It goes into effect any time there is a two hole differential.

pro

n: one who plays golf or teaches golf for money. A professional golfer.

pull

n: a shot that is moving toward the left as a result

(pull cont'd)

of an incorrect swing from outside to in.

push

v: the act of pushing the ball toward its target. The left wrist is not broken but remains firm through the shot which travels low and often has considerable backspin.

Jack Nicklaus

Reading the green

n: a phrase that indicates inspection of the contours and slopes of a green to arrive at a decision about the speed, distance, and direction necessary to putt a ball successfully into a hole.

ready golf

n: in order to speed up play, golfers sometimes play "ready golf" which means that they don't wait to see which player is farthest from the hole, but proceed to strike their ball when they are "ready" to do so.

Red Grange

n: a score of 77 on the tour is a Red Grange, the number that former football star Red Grange wore on his jersey.

red numbers

n: red numbers are used on a scoreboard to show the number of strokes a player is under par. Green numbers are used to denote scores over par. On an electronic display the symbols (–) and (+) are used to denote scores under or over par.

rough

n: areas, usually of long grass adjacent to the tee, fairway, putting green, or hazards. "Short rough," grass cut two to three inches in height, is close to the fairway and "deep rough," where the grass can reach four to six inches in height, is farther away from the fairway.

rounders

n: the act of moving the ball in a circular fashion to the right or left on the green, keeping the same distance from the hole, in order to avoid casual water which lies between the ball and the hole. It is done without penalty.

rut iron

n: a short-headed club, an iron that was developed to enable a golfer to get a ball out of a track or rut. In the early days of golf wagons were used in the maintenance of the course. Their wheels left narrow, deep tracks or ruts. Also called a "track iron."

St. Andrews

n: the "Auld Grey Toon" in Scotland where it all started in the 1500s when Mary, Queen of Scots, played golf there. It was said that she whiffed her first five shots and lost sixteen golf balls on the round. Saint Andrews is not pronounced

Mary, Queen of Scots

the way it looks. Say "Sin Andrus" and the Scots won't know you are a visitor. Originally, St. Andrews had 12 holes. The first 11 traveled straight out to the end of a small peninsula. After playing these the golfers re~ turned to the clubhouse by playing the first 10 greens in reverse order plus a solitary green by the clubhouse. So, originally a "round of golf" consisted of 22 holes at St. Andrews. In 1764, the Royal and Ancient resolved that the first 4 holes should be converted into two and since the same 4 holes became 2 on the way back the "round" was reduced from 22 to 18 holes. Since St. Andrews was the arbiter of all that was correct in golf, 18 holes came to be accepted as the standard of the world.

sand~bagger

n: a hustler who keeps his handicap artifi~ cially high so that he can win tournaments or bets. Also known as a "mug~hunter" be~ cause of the mugs or trophies he collects.

sand trap

n: a hazard in which sand is used — usually a pit whose depth can vary from a foot in a shallow sand trap to as much as 6 to 8 feet in such bunkers as Hell Bunker at St. Andrews. Also called a bunker.

Gene Sarazen

sand wedge

n: a specially constructed club with a broad, low angle face that gives a great deal of loft and with a flange on the bottom that allows the club to slide through the sand under the ball. Gene Sarazen is credited with making the first wedge-type club. The invention of the sand wedge revolutionized sand bunker play.

sandy

n: an "up and down" out of a sand bunker, a blast and then one putt into the cup. When agreed upon in advance, each member of a foursome contributes a specified sum to the player who makes a sandy.

save

n: the act of scoring a par that seems to be in doubt because the player had missed the green and was in the rough at greenside or in a bunker. It is also called "getting up and down," getting on the green and down in one putt.

sclaff

vt: the act of hitting the ground behind the ball before striking the ball— usually with a poor result.

Scotch foursome

n: a game in which two partners take alternate strokes to advance the ball. Sometimes with "selected drives" in which the partners will choose the better drive of the pair.

scramble

n: the name for a modern day game in which all members of a foursome drive and then select the best drive of the foursome for a second shot. All four players then take second shots from that place. That type of play continues un~til the ball is in the hole.

shag

v: the act of retrieving golf balls driven out onto a golf~driving range. Hence, "shag~bag," the bag that holds the prac~tice balls.

shank

v: to strike a ball on the hosel so the ball comes off at a sharp right from the inside curve of the blade or inside curves of the club. It is one of the most disturbing experiences any golfer can ever have. It is also known as a "Chinese lateral," an "out~shoot," or a shot "on the pipe." Even the greatest of golfers have shanked a ball at one time or another. The great Harry Vardon once had the habit so bad that he seriously considered giving up golf for good.

CLANG!

shooting lights out

vt: the act of scoring sensationally well with lots of birdies and eagles, no bogeys. The expression comes from Western movies where the hero in command of the situation shoots out the lights in a saloon.

Don January

skins

n: a game played by three or four golf~ers where the low score on a hole wins the bet provided no other player has the same score. When two players tie for low score, the bet carries over, in effect, doubling the bet for the next hole. An outright win on a hole is called a skin. A win of a carryover that goes three holes is a win of three skins.

Lee Elder

sky

v: to hit under the ball and hit it high but not far. Not unlike a pop-up in baseball.

slice

n: a ball that curves to the right (for a right-handed golfer) because of the clockwise spin imparted to it by the clubhead. Most duffers slice the ball because they do not make a proper turn of the body away from the ball but use only their hands, arms, and upper body. Also called a "banana ball."

smother

v: to close the clubface at impact, that is, rotate the blade in clockwise fashion which lowers the effective loft of the face and causes the ball to take off in a low trajectory to the left.

snake

n: a long putt that finds the bottom of the cup after traveling at least thirty feet over several different breaks in the green. As it heads for the cup it looks like a "snake."

62

socket

n: the opening in the neck of an iron club into which the club shaft is fitted. In Scotland when a player shanks the ball he is said to have "hit it on the socket." In the final round of the British Open of 1932, which he won, Gene Sarazen "socketed one" on an early hole. His caddie put the iron away in the golf bag and said, "We won't be requiring the use of that club anymore, will we, Mr. Sarazen?"

Old Tom Morris

spoon

n: a lofted face fairway wood of early day golf comparable to the 3-wood of today.

spot

v: to mark the position of a ball on the green by placing a coin behind it.

spot putting

n: the act of picking out a discoloration or imper-fection on a green and using that as a target to shoot at on the line to the cup. The spot may be a few inches or a few feet in front of the ball.

stance

n: a player places his feet in position preparatory to making a stroke. He takes a stance.

steel shafts

n: the invention of the steel shaft in the late 1920s

outmoded the old wooden shafts. Steel shafts were more responsive to feel and could be manufactured to consistent tolerances. This made matched sets of clubs possible, matched in weight and flexibility.

steer

vt: to attempt to drive the ball with a stiff wrist action, not a freely released swing. A golfer will try to "steer" the ball when he fears trouble on one side of the hole or the other. Results generally are not good.

stiff

adj: describes a ball hit close to the hole on an approach shot. "He hit it stiff to the pin."

stony

adj: a ball so close to the flagstick that an easy putt will be made. The ball is said to be "stony" or "stone dead."

stymie

n: a ball lying directly in the path of another player's ball on the line to the cup. In the early days of golf, such an obstruction was "played," that is, the ball had to be by-passed or jumped. In the 1930s the rule was finally abandoned. A ball closer than six inches had to be lifted under the stymie rule. Many golf course cards were made exactly six inches long so that a stymie could be measured easily.

sudden death

n: when a medal tournament or the qualifying round

for a tournament ends in a tie between two or more players, they begin a playoff of as many holes are necessary until one player wins a hole and thereby the tournament and the loser is eliminated by "sudden death."

Fuzzy Zoeller, defeated Ed Sneed and Tom Watson in the 1979 Masters.

swing weight

n: the artificially designated physical relationship of clubhead, shaft, overall weight, and club length. A swing weight of C~1, which is light, is suitable for a woman player while a man might use a D~1 to D~5 swing weight.

Take advantage of the flagstick

v: when a player's ball is not on the putting surface he has the right to ask that the flagstick be left in the hole. Sometimes this can work to the golfer's advantage especially on a slippery downhill approach. Hitting the flagstick may help to stop the ball near the cup, might even allow it to fall into the hole.

take it

v: when your opponent says "take it," it means that he is conceding your next putt—also "pick it up" and "that's good." It also means "take the flagstick" out of the hole.

tap~in

n: a very short putt usually of no more than a few

inches which can be tapped lightly into the cup. Holing a "tap~in" is not a certainty, however. Hale Irwin went to tap in a 2~inch putt in the 1984 British Open and whiffed the ball. He lost the championship by a single stroke. Even the great Arnold Palmer has been known to miss a tap~in.

tee

n: the specially designed close~cropped area from which the first shot on a hole is taken. The marker for the tee is on a horizontal line perpendicular to the line to the hole. The golfer may tee his ball any~where in the rectangle formed by the line between the markers and a line two club~lengths depth be~hind the markers.

Also, the wooden peg on which the ball is placed before it is struck from the tee area.

temporary green

n: in winter and early spring or when greens are under repair, temporary greens are often mowed out of the fairway grass near the permanent green in order to protect the regular green from abuse. Temporary greens are usually rough and difficult to putt on successfully.

that dog will hunt

an expression that indicates an es~pecially long straight drive down the fairway.

that's good

statement: what your opponent says when he

concedes your putt. When this happens, reach down and pick up the ball quickly for if you attempt to putt it you surely will miss.

three~fifty club

n: a club comprised of some of the world's longest hitters. To qualify for the group, a golfer must have driven the ball more than 350 yards in a long drive competition.

tiger tees

n: the tees that are far~thest away from the hole are said to be deep in "tiger country." The Scot~tish name for "Blue tees" or Championship tees. Country club members in the U.S. usually play from white tees and women from yellow tees even closer to the green.

Everybody's a critic!

tight lie

n: a lie in which the ball sits right on a bare or bald spot where there is no grass at all.

top

vt: to hit the ball above the middle and hit a poor shot that travels a short distance.

turn

v: after a golfer finishes the 9th hole and proceeds to the 10th, he is said to "make the turn." This expres~

sion stems from the early days of golf when the first nine holes went "out" and the second nine went "in" toward the clubhouse.

Also, an expression of body movement away from the ball in the backswing. The greater the turn, the more power generated.

two~ball

n: a golf event in which two partners play together against another pair of golfers. Scoring in a two~ball event is varied—low ball of the pair, combined total of the pair, low ball and low total of the pair.

two~club wind

n: a twenty miles per hour wind that affects the distance a ball will travel. A 5~iron with a two~club wind will have the effect of a 3~iron. A 5~iron against a two~club wind will have the effect of a 7~iron.

Waggle

v: moving the clubhead back and forth over the ball in preparation for a swing. Cary Middle~coff, Masters and U.S. Open Champion, was known to waggle as many as twenty~four times before he struck the ball.

whiff

v: to miss the ball completely, to "fan"

Cary Middlecoff

(whiff cont'd)

the ball. The expression is believed to have originated in 1876 when Lord Gormley Whiffle completely missed a 4~inch putt to lose the Silver Medal at St. Andrews Old Course by one stroke. The spectators kept remarking to one another, "Did you see that Whiffle?" Later the phrase was shortened to its present form.

Hale Irwin

whipping

n: strong black twine used as a tight wrapping to attach a wooden shafted club to its hosel.

wind~cheater

n: a ball which is hit on a lower than normal tra~jectory in order to lessen the effect of a head wind.

winter rules

n: a local rule providing for the lifting and cleaning of a ball lying in the fairway and placing it within six inches of where it originally lay, but not nearer the hole.

woods

n: the name given to wooden~headed golf clubs. The driver is the #1 wood and customarily golfers of to~day carry three or four wood clubs in their bag, the #3 (with greater loft) and the #5 (with even more loft). Older golfers sometimes carry a #7 wood. The ori~ginal names for the woods were driver, brassie, spoon, and baffy or cleek.

Yips

   n: an unfortunate nerve condition which affects the muscles of the hands and wrists on short putts. Golfers with a bad case of the yips have been known to knock a 3~foot putt fifteen feet beyond the hole. Ben Hogan's golf career came to an end primarily because of a bad case of the yips.

NICKNAMES

Severiano (Seve) Ballesteros

This handsome young Spaniard has made a major impact on international golf. He has won the Masters twice, in 1980 and in 1983 and the 1979 and 1984 British Open tournaments. Seve is known for his long and occasionally wild drives along with remarkable ability to recover from impossible spots in the rough.

Miller (Mr. X) Barber

A bachelor for many years who hid behind huge dark sunglasses, he was called "Mr. X" because he fled town quickly after cashing big golf checks. Miller has hit the senior circuit with a bang. He picked up nearly $300,000 in 1984 after making a million and a half for himself on the main tour.

Tommy (The Terrible Tempered Mr. Bang) Bolt

His fiery temperament and inclination to throw clubs when he was angry got him his nickname. He won the 1958 U.S. Open, defeating Gary Player by four strokes.

71

Julius (Moose) Boros

Because he has a wide face and looks a little bit like one, friends called him "Moose." He is also called "Big Julie" and "Old Man River" because of his ambling, easy-going gait and relaxed attitude.

JoAnne (Big Momma) Carner

She is a big woman, 5 feet, 7 inches tall, solidly built, and is the friendly "Momma" to all other women on the LPGA tour. As an amateur she was called "The Great Gundy" when she won five U.S. Amateur championships because her maiden name was Gunderson.

Billy (Buffalo Bill) Casper

Because he had severe allergies to pesticides and to certain foods, his doctors recommended he eat no meat other than buffalo. Billy lost a lot of weight on the diet, which he has regained, and then some, but the nickname stuck. An excellent golfer, he has earned more than one-and-one-half million dollars in prize money by winning 51 tournaments, including U.S. Opens in 1959 and 1966 and the Masters in 1970.

Robert D. (Harpo) Clampett

He looks like Harpo Marx with his shock of curly blond hair.

Harry (Light Horse) Cooper

Because he had a fast swing and moved quickly, they called him Light Horse Harry. He was a top player in the 1920s and 1930s who almost won several big tournaments.

Fred (Boom Boom) Couples

His drives go off like cannon shots for distances frequently farther than 300 yards, so they call Couples "Boom Boom."

Ben (Gentle Ben) Crenshaw

Crenshaw is called "Gentle Ben" be~ cause he is soft~spoken, self~effacing, and always gracious. One of the best putters in modern day golf, he holed a monstrous snake on the 11th at Augusta in 1984 to help him win his first Masters title.

Robert (Wee Bobby) Cruickshank

Called "Wee Bobby" because he was only 5~feet 5~inches tall, Cruickshank was a great player of the 1930s, was twice runner~up for the U.S. Open, once to Jones in 1923 and once to Sarazen in 1932.

Dave (Eagleberger) Eichelberger

In 1980 Dave scored more eagles (16) than anyone

(Dave Eichelberger cont'd)
else on the PGA tour. Not only that, but he had two of
them at Tallahassee where he won his fourth PGA title.

C. L. (Gibby) Gilbert

Gibby is C.L. Gilbert, Jr. Oddly, he
has no first or middle names, just the
initials. His father C.L. Gilbert,
Sr., also only has initials for
a name. The father is known as
Gil and the son has been known as Gibby all his
life. He's won three championships and nearly a million
dollars on the tour.

...But you can call me "GIBBY"

Don (Tex) January

A slim 6~foot Texan who has had 27 tour victories
during a long and very successful 28 years of campaign~
ing, Don has won nearly two million dollars. His biggest
victory came in the 1967 PGA championship at Columbine
Country Club. He was also a member of the 1965 and 1977
Ryder Cup Teams. Since he became a senior player he has
been winning more than ever, and has
won over a million dollars.

Bernhard (The Red Baron) Langer

Because he comes from Germany and
is a golfing ace, Langer
has been nicknamed
The Red Baron after the first Red
Baron, Manfred von Richtofen, World
War I German flying ace. Langer
wears solid red clothes on the golf tour.
Langer (pronounced LAHNGER)

captured the 1985 Masters in sensational fashion, coming from behind to overtake the leaders in the final round.

Gene (The Machine) Littler

Because of his smooth, effortless grooved swing that never varies in its tempo, Gene Littler was called "The Machine." In 1961 he won the U.S. Open at Oakland Hills and became the eighth person to win both the Open and the U.S. Amateur. He has won 28 tour tournaments and more than 2 million dollars in his lifetime.

William (Wild Bill) Mehlhorn

He was a crowd~pleasing regular on the PGA tour in the 1920s and 1930s. Mehlhorn got his nickname because he wore colorful cowboy hats, talked a lot, and behaved un~ conventionally. One time he perched high in a tree and needled Bobby Cruickshank as Bobby tried to make a thousand dollar putt.

Orville (The Sarge) Moody

Famous for the one and only tour victory in his life, the United States Open of 1969 at the Champions Golf Club in Texas, Moody had been a staff sergeant for 14 years in the army. He is known for his cross~handed putting stroke, which does not work very well, and for his statement, "I never practice golf. All it does is louse up my game."

Greg (The Great White Shark) Norman

His white tow~head, his sharp beak of a nose, and the fact that he used to hunt sharks under the reefs of the Australian coast~

line led to his nickname. Norman was second in the 1984 U.S. Open to Fuzzy Zoeller, and won two tournaments in 1984.

Edward (Porky) Oliver

A jovial, rotund man, Oliver was never a major tournament winner, but a runner~up in the 1946 PGA and the 1953 Masters. His full nickname was "Pork Chops" because he used to order them for break~ fast. Renowned for a score of 16 he made on the 16th hole, a 222~yard par~3 at Cypress Point during the 1954 Crosby Tournament. Porky put four balls into the ocean, went down on the beach to continue the battle, finally sinking a putt on his sixteenth stroke.

Masahi (Jumbo) Ozaki

Tall and muscular, one of the greatest Japanese players of all time, he could hit the ball a country mile. He was called "Jumbo" because he was unusually large for a Japanese.

Barbara (L'il Tiger) Romack

Although she's tiny, not over 5~feet 3~inches, she's a tiger who never let her opponent get away from her. In 1954 she won the U.S. Amateur championship in a final match that took 29½ hours to play because of intermit~ tent thundershowers.

Paul (Little Poison) Runyan

Paul Runyan was called "Little Poison" because al~ though he was physically small, only about 5~feet 6~ inches tall, and slight, he was absolute murder to his opponents. He slaughtered Sam Snead in the finals of the

1938 PGA championship 8 and 6, consistently putting his 5-wood second shots inside Snead's iron shots to the greens.

Horton (The Joplin Ghost) Smith

Because he is tall, unassuming, inobtrusive, quiet, and born in Joplin, Missouri, Smith was called "The Joplin Ghost." He was the greatest putter of the 1930s and the winner of two Masters titles, 1934 and 1936. They also called him "The Velvet Touch" because of his delicate putting stroke that invariably found the hole.

Hollis (Spacey) Stacy

She won the USGA Girls championship for three consecutive years. As a professional she has won three LPGA Opens. Stacy is one of the tour's most flamboyant performers who loves rock and roll dancing. She is called "Spacey" because she always seems to be somewhere else than the space she's occupying at the moment.

Craig (The Walrus) Stadler

Craig's weight varies between 250 and 190 pounds, but he plays marvelous golf at any weight, ambling along in a bearlike shuffle with his belt anchored several inches below his ample belly. His nickname is obviously appropriate, and to top off the image, he has a big bushy moustache. The 1982 Masters was his first major championship and in that year he was the leading money winner on the PGA tour with a total of $446,442.

Lee (The Merry Mex) Trevino

A genial, talkative Texan of Mexican heritage, Trevino sports a suitable nickname. Trevino's major victories are the U.S. Open in 1968, two British Open championships, and two PGA championships, the most recent in 1984.

Frank Urban (Fuzzy) Zoeller

Zoeller's nickname comes from the initials of his name: F.U.Z. A real character of modern day golf, colorful, talkative, he won the Masters Tournament in 1979 after a playoff with Ed Sneed and Tom Watson. Fuzzy is noted for his unusual swing with hands held low and for placing the clubhead outside his line and then drawing it into the ball before making his swing.

Lee Trevino

HARRY VARDON

One of the best players of all time, Harry Vardon (1870-1937) also was most responsible for making golf popular in its early days. Along with James Braid and John Henry Taylor, Vardon dominated the game in the years between 1896 and 1914. He won six British Open Championships, a record which still stands. He was also runner-up four times and third twice. Most golfers believe he was the originator of the "Vardon Grip" (he was not, J.H. Taylor was), which featured the little finger of the right hand overlapping the forefinger of the left hand for greater compactness.

Vardon was so accurate a wood player that it was said that on his second round of the day, he would find himself in the middle of the fairway hitting out of the divots he had made on his first round.

Vardon came to the United States at the height of his career and won the U.S. Open Championship in 1900. He also came close to winning the U.S. Open again when he tied for the title with young (twenty-year-old) Francis Ouimet of the United States along with Edward "Ted" Ray, long-driving fellow British star. Ouimet won that playoff in dramatic fashion on the demanding Brookline course, The Country Club, outside of Boston in 1913.

Vardon won the last of his opens in 1914, eighteen years after his first which was a tribute to his sound consistent swing. Vardon's style was especially rhythmic and graceful and appeared to be effortless. He played from an open stance, that is, with his left foot drawn back from the line of flight, and oddly, he violated the rule of modern day golf instructions by breaking his left arm in his back swing. Of course, he straightened it on the forward swing. He played with shorter and lighter clubs than the other good players of his era and was considered a long driver by his fellow competitors.

Vardon was 5-feet 9-inches tall and carried ten wooden-shafted

clubs, two of which were spares for his driver and brassie. Shafts broke easily in those days and the heads would fly off at unexpected times.

Vardon was called a golfing genius by Bernard Darwin, the leading golf writer of that era. Vardon was so accurate with his long shots to the green that he rarely had to use his niblick to make his approach. His temperament was serene and he played with "gallant courage" most confidently. He was a true "gentleman golfer", most considerate of his opponent's feelings.

Three of Vardon's six championships were won with the hard "guttie" ball and three were won after the introduction of the rubber-cored Haskell ball. Vardon was considered a good putter but not a great one. It was said that if he had been a great putter he would have been undefeated in major competition for fifteen years.

In January 1900 Vardon toured the United States and played matches nearly every day. It was this tour that brought golf to the attention of the multitude of Americans who, until that time, considered golf a rich man's pastime, an effete sport.

They saw a real he-man striking the golf ball prodigious distances and they began to want to participate in this then novel sport.

JOHN HENRY TAYLOR

The third member, along with Harry Vardon and James Braid, of the "Great Triumvirate" of golf, John Henry Taylor (1871-1963) was a master of the mashie (today's 5-iron) and with this club could make the ball do tricks. The mashie then had deep grooves in its face markings that would be illegal in today's game.

Playing with Englishman Taylor in America one time, Bobby Jones complimented him on a particularly good drive whereupon Taylor barked, "What did you expect?" and finished the round without saying another word.

"J.H.", a dour, shy man won the British Open five times—1894, 1895, 1900, 1909, and 1913. He was runner-up in 1896, 1906, and tied for the runner-up spot in 1904 and 1905. He was also runner-up in the U.S. Open of 1900 losing to his perennial rival Harry Vardon.

Taylor began as a caddie at Westward Ho! in England and at the age of seventeen became an assistant green-keeper. Of course, he could and did play all the golf he wanted to and his skill bought him to the attention of the better golfers. Soon he was challenged by famous Andrew Kirkaldy of St. Andrews. He beat Kirkaldy and later succeeded him as professional at the Winchester Club in Surrey, England. Taylor moved to Royal Mid-Surrey where he stayed for more than forty years.

Taylor was a stern competitor and approached every championship as if it were a battle. He had a strong firm-footed stance and a short punched swing. He could drive the ball low and with great accuracy. Nobody else could match his compact stroke. One of his greatest victories in the Open came at Hoylake in appalling wind and rain. He pulled his cap down tightly over his ears, planted his sturdy hobnailed boots firmly in the ground and drove the ball straight through the wind as if it were not there.

J.H. had no less than ten holes-in-one in his long distinguished career. The most opportune one came at famous old Prestwick in the 1925 British Open Championship, the tournament won by "Long Jim" Barnes of the United States. Taylor's hole-in-one enabled him to tie for fifth in the tournament.

Taylor was a bold player in a day of conservative golf. He was one of the first to challenge the deep bunkers in front of the greens rather than play safe by hitting short and then using his niblick to the green. He was not as long a driver as Vardon, but he was Vardon's equal in steadiness and accuracy.

Taylor was so shy that once, when his club members wanted to give a party for him, to celebrate one of his championships, he deliberately took the train to a stop past the golf club, walked back over the moors to his house so he would not be seen and therefore would not have to go to the party.

In 1957 the Royal North Devon paid him the highest honor of his life by electing him president. He lived to the ripe old age of 92.

JAMES BRAID

The third member of the "Great Triumvirate," James "Big Jim" Braid (1870-1950), was a Scot. Together with Harry Vardon and J.H. Taylor, the three golfers dominated British golf from 1874 to World War I. Among them they shared sixteen British Open championships. Braid won five—1901, 1905, 1906, 1908, and 1910. Braid's record score for the British Open, a 291 in 1908, stood up for nineteen years until Robert T. "Bobby" Jones, Jr., broke it in 1927. Although Big Jim was a tall, slim man, he was not an unusually long hitter for most of his career. Then suddenly, almost overnight, he discovered the secret of long driving and from then on was known as one of the longest drivers of golf. Braid also had thirteen holes-in-one in his long career. Braid later became a renowned golf course designer. He is probably most famous for building the classic Gleneagles Kings Course in Scotland. It is said that he strolled over the hills and through the heather and planted spikes, apparently at random, saying, "We'll have a green here, a tee there." The result was one of the greatest and most picturesque courses in the world.

He came from a humble background—the son of a ploughman. His father, who never played golf, was unsympathetic to James's ambitions on the links and to his desire to become a professional golfer. Braid left school at the age of thirteen and became a journeyman carpenter, but managed to play in amateur golf events in his home area. After he won an amateur title in his early twenties, he was encouraged to turn professional and he went to London as an apprentice club-maker.

All golf clubs were made by hand and there was a growing demand for good clubmakers. His pay at first was eight pence an hour, but later on his salary was raised to a shilling (twelve cents).

Braid played golf in the evenings after work and soon developed

an individual style. He had a full swing "with a very loose knee (the left) when he really went after the ball." It was said that he played with "a divine fury."

By 1895 Braid started to make his mark in golf. He tied J.H. Taylor in an important match at West Drayton. By 1901 Braid had won his first British Open Championship.

By that time J.H. Taylor and Vardon had each won the title three times. Within a few years Braid became the first man to win the Open Championship five times, although Taylor equalled this record later and Vardon surpassed it. To put in perspective the marvelous golfing feats of Braid, Taylor, and Vardon, it is informative to note that in the modern era only Peter Thomson and Tom Watson have won the title five times.

Braid was in great demand as a golf course architect. Many a Scottish course today is proud of a Braid design and, according to the custom of giving holes distinctive names, the most difficult hole on a course will often bear the Braid name—"Braid's Brawest" (toughest). Once in a while a hole may be called, "Braid's Folly," a name that connotes the fact that some club members thought Braid had created a poorly designed hole.

At the age of seventy, James Braid was honored by the Royal and Ancient Golf Club of St. Andrews by being named an honorary member. Braid died at the age of eighty. He was a reserved man, an immensely painstaking man of few words.

WALTER HAGEN

One of the most colorful golfers of all time, Walter "The Haig" Hagen (1892-1969), was the first professional golfer allowed to enter the front door of swank country clubs. Once that happened the standing of all professional golfers improved from "tradesmen" to "gentlemen". He had broken the class barrier, and it stayed broken from then on.

Walter had a slashing swing with a pronounced forward sway, but he could make every shot in the bag. He was noted for his showmanship. He would often pretend that a shot was very difficult and take a great deal of time to survey it. Then he would execute it successfully with a smile and great flair.

Hagen won eleven national championships, four British Opens, two United States Opens, and five PGA championships. The PGA was conducted at match play in the 1920s when The Haig was at the peak of his ability. He won twenty-two straight matches in the PGA tourneys, an unmatchable feat and one that will never be equalled now that the event has become a medal play event.

Hagen played about 1,500 exhibitions all over the world. Before he would start, he would ask some knowledgeable person what the course record was for the links he was about to attack, and then he would bet huge sums of money that he could beat it. In nearly all cases he did.

On one occasion Hagen had bet he would break the course record of 67 at a particular course. A large gallery was following him as he came to the eighteenth green. He needed to sink a twenty-five foot putt to break the record and win the bet.

The crowd was hushed and expectant as he bent over the ball. There wasn't a sound, not even a whisper. Then Hagen suddenly stopped, looked up, and said to the crowd, "Is there anybody here who thinks I'm not going to make this putt?" The tension was broken, of course. Then The Haig did sink the putt and won the bets. Hagen hauled away his winnings and the gate receipts in a suit case.

When Robert T. "Bobby" Jones was in his prime, Hagen played Jones four successive rounds of match play in a challenge match, "the World's Greatest Pro vs. the World's Greatest Amateur." He defeated Jones 12 and 11, the worst trouncing Jones ever took.

Melvin "Chick" Harbert (later PGA Champion himself in 1954) was a boy wonder of golf in Michigan in the 1930s. When Hagen visited the Benton Harbor area, young Harbert, seventeen years old, was invited to play in an exhibition of golf against Hagen. Chick relates the story, "I was nervous at first playing against the great golfer, but finally I settled down and when we came to the 18th hole we were even. We were both on the par-4 green in two strokes. I was a little farther away than the Haig, about fifteen feet to his ten.

"Very carefully I surveyed my putt. I circled to the left, I circled to the right. I got down on my hands and knees behind the ball. Then I stepped up and sank the putt for the birdie I thought would beat Hagen.

"He accepted the situation calmly. He circled to the right, he circled to the left, he even got down on his hands and knees mimicking exactly every move I had made. Then he stepped up to his putt and knocked it into the hole *backhanded*!"

Hagen was a master at the psychology of golf and frequently would attempt to mislead his opponent about his club selection. Al Watrous, great golfer of the 1920s, runner-up to Bobby Jones in the British Open of 1921 at Royal Lytham and St. Anne's, told this story about Hagen. They were playing in the 1925 PGA Championship at Olympia Fields in Chicago, and came to the eighteenth hole, a dangerous par-5 with water in front of the green. The match was tied. Watrous's ball was in the fairway, Hagen's was in the woods to the left. Watrous was away so he had to play first for the green. He could see Walter brandishing a wood club in a practice swing in the rough. That meant that Hagen had a good lie and would be able to go for the green with his second shot. Watrous thought if Hagen was going to use a wood so would he, and when he did he put his ball in the water. Then Hagen pulled out an iron, which he had been intending to use all along, played safely to the fairway and then to the green in three to win the match from Watrous.

Hagen was never known to stoop to pick up a golf tee. After he had driven he would stride off determinedly down the fairway and the gallery would rush to pick up a Hagen souvenir.

Walter loved wine and women, not necessarily in that order. And sometimes in his big touring car he would arrive at a golf course still wearing his tuxedo from the night before. He had been up all night, but that didn't matter. He would change his shoes, put on his fresh white linen knickers and be ready to play in his own good time. He never hurried and was always late. That was "The Haig."

One time Hagen was partying strongly at 2 A.M. when one of his friends told him, "Your opponent for tomorrow has been in bed since ten o'clock." Hagen replied, "Yeah, but he's not sleeping!"

Hagen at one time lived in splendor at the Detroit Athletic Club, a plush men's club famous for its cuisine. The Haig's weight got up to the 300 pound mark. His customary breakfast at 1:00 P.M. was two broiled Maine lobsters (according to one of the DAC waiters who served him).

Hagen dressed in the finest clothes and drove the best of cars. He made a million dollars in his long successful career and he spent most of the money. His motto in life was, "You're only here for a short visit. Don't hurry. Don't worry. And be sure to smell the flowers along the way."

ROBERT T. JONES, JR.

ROBERT T. JONES, JR.

At the age of 28, Robert T. "Bobby" Jones, Jr. (1902-1971) accomplished "the greatest exhibition of skill and character by any individual athlete, bar none, since the beginning of sports history." He won the British Amateur, the British Open, the United States Open, and the United States Amateur Championships all in the same year—the Grand Slam.

Jones hated the name, Bobby, and was always called Bob by his friends. But the Scots who loved him with a passion dubbed him Bobby and to the rest of the world he remained Bobby all his life. In the 1920s it was Jones who dominated the field in the U.S.Open and U.S. Amateur Championships just as it was Ben Hogan in the 1950s and Jack Nicklaus in the 1960s.

Jones, an attorney-at law by profession, came from a well-to-do family and never played any game but golf. He thought that this focused effort was one of the reasons for his success.

Jones was called the boy wonder of golf. He won the Georgia State Amateur championship when he was only fourteen years old. He also qualified for the U.S. Amateur that year. When he was only seventeen, he was runner-up in three major championships, the Southern Open, the Canadian Open, and the U.S. National Amateur Championship. For a while it appeared that he would be a perpetual runner-up but he broke through in 1920 to win the Southern Amateur. He was medalist in the National Amateur, and played respectably in the U.S. Open, finishing in eighth place.

He moved up to second place in the 1922 U.S. Open and again in the Southern Amateur. At last, in 1923 he won his first U.S. Open, defeating Bobby Cruickshank in a playoff, 76 to 78 at Inwood on Long Island. From then on, there was no stopping him. It was Jones against the field until 1930. He won: the U.S. Open again in 1926,

1929, and 1930; the Amateur in 1924, 1925, 1927, 1928, and 1930; the British Open in 1926, 1927, and 1930; and the British Amateur in 1930. Jones had won thirteen National Championships in only seven years. In the U.S. Amateur he was either winner or runner-up every year from 1924 to 1930 and in the U.S. Open he was either first or second every year, except one from 1922 to 1930.

Jones was only 5-feet 8-inches tall and inclined to be stout. He had a full, fluid, graceful swing that appeared to be so leisurely that the great distances he hit the ball came as a surprise. He was an excellent putter and used an old wooden shafter blade he called "Calamity Jane." It was made for him by master club-maker Tom Stewart in Scotland.

After he won the "Impregnable Quadrilateral" (as the four tournaments were dubbed by sportswriter Grantland Rice), Jones felt that he had accomplished everything he possibly could do in golf. The stress of tournament play took a grievous toll on his nerves and body. He could never keep his breakfast down on the morning of a crucial match. He would lose from seven to ten pounds over the course of a four-day tournament.

A lucrative contract—a million dollars—was offered him by the Spalding Company, premier maker of golf clubs and other sports equipment. It meant that Bobby would have to relinquish his amateur standing and become a professional in the eyes of the United States Golf Association. He accepted the proposal and soon Spalding began to manufacture new Robert T. Jones, Jr. models of golf clubs. The golfing public bought them by the millions. Jones also made some very successful movie shorts that demonstrated his swing, club by club.

Jone's next endeavor was the building of the Augusta National Golf Club at Augusta, Georgia. He envisioned a golf club composed of prominent members from all over the country, from all over the world, an invited group of golf enthusiasts who would play on one of the finest golf courses in the world. Famed Scottish designer, Donald McKenzie worked with Jones and turned a former nursery in the magnificent rolling countryside into the Augusta National Golf Club, one of the most gloriously beautiful courses in the world.

Next, Jones invited a few of his friends to an Invitational Tournament at the club in spring when the azaleas and dogwood were in bloom. From that small group there evolved an annual get-together which came to be called the Masters Tournament, for it was clear that Jones was inviting the masters of golf to play in his tournament every year.

In the meantime Jones had contracted a seriously debilitating spinal disease. Until his death in 1971 he suffered a slow and painful deterioration of his body. His mind remained bright and alert and he was always cheerful, never admitting to anyone that he was in pain.

In the early days of the Masters, Jones would always participate in the tournament, though his golfing skills were no longer good enough to keep up with the stars of those days—Gene Sarazen, Craig Wood, Horton Smith, Ralph Guldahl, and others.

It was the custom each year that Jones would play with the previous year's winner in the first round. So it happened that in 1929 Henry Picard (winner of the Masters in 1938) was playing with Jones as they came to the 9th hole, a 420-yard par-4 with an elevated green that slopes severely from back to front. Jones's second shot went just over the back edge of the green. Picard said to Jones, "I'll bet you the clubhouse you can't keep your chip-shot on the green." Jones scoffed at Picard.

Picard said, "His chip-shot rolled down the green and right off the front of it. The next year the green was flattened out."

In 1958 the first World Amateur Golf Team Championship was, most fittingly, played at the "Old Course" at St. Andrews, Scotland. Jones, then seriously ailing, was named Captain of the American team.

By then he was using a wheel chair, but he determined to make one last pilgrimage to old St. Andrews and the charming Scottish people he loved so well. Shortly before he left for Scotland, he was asked whether he would accept "the Freedom of the City" while he was there. He knew it would be an honor, but did not know precisely what was involved. He accepted the invitation.

The presentation ceremony was held at the Younger Graduation Hall of St. Andrews University and was attended by 1,700 enthusiasts. Jones was driven up the aisle of the Hall in a golf cart (the only one allowed at St. Andrews) and then he climbed the stairs to the stage with the help of a hickory-shafted cane.

In his presentation speech Provost Robert Leonard told Jones, "We welcome you back as an old and dearly loved friend, as an amabassador in the cause of international understanding and good will."

Jones was told that among the privileges he would have in the future were, "the right to cast shells, to take divots, and to dry his washing on the first and last fairways of the Old Course." He was also named a Burgess and Guild Brother of the City of St. Andrews. The last American before Jones to be so honored was Benjamin Franklin, 199 years earlier.

As Jones left the auditorium, the assemblage broke out softly into the old Scottish song, "Will Ye No' Come Back Again?" and there was not a dry eye in the house because Jones knew and everyone else knew, too, that he would never come back again.

GENE SARAZEN

Gene Sarazen is one of golf's all-time leading lights, with one of the longest careers in any sport. He is one of only four players who have won all four of the major professional tournaments, the U.S. Open in 1922 and 1932, the British Open in 1932, the PGA Championship in 1922, 1923, and 1933, and the Masters in 1935.

Gene's father was a carpenter who as a young man in Italy, had studied to be a priest before he came to America. When Gene was young, he worked as an apprentice to his father and also caddied to earn extra money at the nearby Apawamis Club. Gene was only eight years old when he started, so diminutive and so likeable that the members of the club went out of their way to see that he did not have to carry a heavy bag.

As Gene grew older he spent as much time as he could on the golf course. His father frowned on Gene's golf aspirations. When Gene had an attack of pleurisy and the doctor's advice was for him to get out of the dusty carpentry shop and work in the open air, Gene became an assistant professional at Brooklawn Country Club in Connecticut. He had a natural swing and a marvelous sense of rhythm and balance. Although only 5-feet 5½-inches tall, Sarazen had a stocky frame, strong hands and arms, and sturdy legs. He could drive a ball straight and far with the best of them.

When Gene was only eighteen, he was encouraged to enter the 1920 U.S. Open at Inverness in Toledo, Ohio. He played very well, qualified third, and finished thirtieth. Two years later, at twenty, he became the youngest U.S. Open champion of all time when he won at Lakeville in Flushing, Long Island.

Gene is famous for several remarkable golf feats. The one the public remembers most is undoubtedly, "the shot that was heard around the world." It happened in the second Masters tournament in 1935.

Bobby Jones had invited sixty-three of his friends, the best golfers in the world to play in his Invitational Tournament at the Augusta National Golf Course. Not for several more years would the tournament be called the Masters. Sarazen started off with a 68 to Craig Wood's 69. The next day Gene shot 71 to Craig's 72 but on the third round Wood roared back with a 68 to Gene's 73. On the fateful last day Gene started three strokes behind Craig Wood who was playing in front of him.

When Sarazen reached the 485-yard par-5 fifteenth hole, he was still three strokes behind Wood. Gene knew that Wood was in the clubhouse with a last round of 73. Gene had to shoot a score of three-under par on the last four holes in order to tie Wood. It was apparently an impossible task because those last four holes are extremely difficult and demanding.

Gene drove 265 yards on the fifteenth hole and landed in the fairway. The fairway is high on this hole and from where his drive had stopped Gene could look down on the green in the distant shadows.

Sarazen turned away from his ball in the wet fairway grass and peered down the long slope to the green, 220 yards away. A freezing wind disturbed the flag and ripped through his protective sweater. Around him, one thousand eyewitnesses huddled together in a crescent that bulged behind the green and thinned out to a single line on either side of the fairway.

Before the green lay a pond—not much of a pond, really—perhaps forty feet across at its broadest. It protected the green, yet it could be an easy birdie for a player who could put together two excellent wood shots and was willing to gamble.

Gene Sarazen was that gambler. He reached for his favored 4-wood, took another quick glimpse ahead through the mist, and swung.

He watched the ball as well as he could as it sailed up into the haze and over the pond to the fifteenth green. It dropped on the apron, popped up twice on the turf, and rolled relentlessly toward the cup as though homing in on a magnet. A thousand voices in the gallery screamed as the ball disappeared into the cup for a double-eagle-2.

Gene Sarazen strode down the remaining two hundred yards of

fairway between the two lines of shouting fans like a king walking to his throne, the 4-wood held in front of him like a scepter. "It was the greatest thrill I have ever had on a golf course," he said. "I realized all I needed now was par to tie."

Gene parred the last three holes and tied Craig Wood. The next day in a 36-hole playoff, Sarazen beat Wood by five strokes.

The second incredible performance by Sarazen happened in the 1932 U.S. Open, which was held at Fresh Meadow Country Club in New York. Gene had been pro there for six seasons, but he felt superstitious about a home pro trying to win an Open on his own course. He didn't want to be jinxed, so he changed jobs to nearby Lakeville. He won the British Open that year and came physically tired to the U.S. Open two weeks later. In those days, the last thirty-six holes of the U.S. Open were played on the same day, so those holes were consecutive. After the first eight holes of his third round Gene stood seven strokes behind the leader, Phil Perkins. Then Gene got hot. There has never been such a streak of low scoring in golf since he set Fresh Meadow afire that day. Gene played the final twenty-eight holes in 100 strokes. That is an average of 3.6 storkes per hole. When he finished he had won with 286 strokes, three strokes ahead of Perkins and Bobby Cruickshank.

For those last twenty-eight holes Gene had four 2's, seven 3's, fourteen 4's and only three 5's. He had a total of nine birdies! In the early days golfers had great difficulty getting the ball out of sand traps. The club would dig into the sand and lose all its force. Gene had the inspired idea of making a club that would skid under the ball instead of digging in. He experimented and developed the first sand wedge with a flange on its bottom so it could skim under the ball and "explode" it from the sand more easily. With his new golfing tool in hand, it was said that Gene would often deliberately shoot for the sand traps because he knew he could get "up and down" in two strokes.

Gene is called "The Squire" or "The Country Squire" because a number of years ago he took some of his substantial winnings and bought a farm in upper New York and became a gentleman farmer.

Sarazen has always been an advocate of playing golf fast. Like Bobby Cruickshank, he believes in the old adage, "Miss 'em quick." Sarazen and George Fazio played the last round of the 1947 Masters in one hour and fifty-seven minutes. Sarazen's score was 70.

Gene is also well-known for his golfing attire. He always wears knickers on the golf course. He has had hundreds of pairs specially made for him and is partly responsible for current interest in the traditional golf attire of the early 1900s.

In the 1950s Gene was playing with an amateur partner, an automobile dealer, who was using golf clubs that were about ten years old. When Gene saw them, he said, "Would you drive a car that's ten years old? They have improved golf clubs as much as they've improved cars." The amateur went out the next day and bought a new set of Sarazen clubs.

Gene officially retired from tournament golf after playing in the 1973 British Open. He created a sensation there when, with television cameras rolling, he scored a remarkable hole-in-one on Troon's famous 126-yard eighth hole, "The Postage Stamp."

Gene always attends the Masters tournament in early April to renew friendships with all his old golfing rivals, Sam Snead, Byron Nelson, Jerry Barber, Cary Middlecoff, Jack Burke, Jr., and Paul Runyan. Gene can be seen sitting on the porch of the old Georgian clubhouse holding court before his many admirers, undoubtedly retelling the story once again of the double-eagle-2 in 1935.

Gene now lives in southern Florida and still plays golf with great skill several times a week. One of the golf courses at PGA headquarters was recently named, "The Squire" and dedicated to him in recognition of his international reputation and his gentlemanly character.

The plaque at PGA headquarters reads, "Gene Sarazen set standards in golf. He was a true competitor who became the first to win the Professional Grand Slam. He attacked golf courses with an unharnessed fury. His style of golf is legendary. His character, his charisma, and his charges won him a legion of followers throughout the world."

BEN HOGAN

Ben Hogan is regarded as the greatest shot-maker of the modern era, possibly the best golfer of all time. Jack Nicklaus is the only player who has come close to the perfection and dominance of the game that Hogan achieved in his prime.

Gene Sarazen has said, "Nobody covered the flag the way Hogan did." Hogan, not a big man at 5-feet 7-inches, weighed only 138 pounds. He was leading money-winner in 1940, about $13,000 in prize money. Compare that amount with the $436,000 Tom Watson earned in 1984!

Hogan was called "The Hawk" because his grey eyes had the piercing steely look of a hawk. He smiled rarely and was all business when he played. He usually wore a white linen visored cap and smoked incessantly. The Scots admired his marvelous play at Carnoustie in 1953 when he won the Open. They dubbed him, "the Wee Ice Mon", a nickname which fitted Ben even more than The Hawk, for he was a cold man.

Hogan was a ruthless perfectionist. He hit thousands of golf balls day after day on the practice tee trying to find the secret of the perfect swing. Ben hooked badly in his early days, a sudden darting right-to-left duck hook. He said, "When I hook I get nauseated."

Ben figured out a way to avoid any possibility of his dreaded hook. He taught himself never to let the clubface close at impact and developed a gentle, accurate right-to-left fade.

Hogan became so accurate with his swing that he could put the ball down on a bedsheet 250 yards down the fairway twenty times in a row. He was a strong competitor who tried to birdie every hole. Ben once said, "If you can't birdie the first hole how can you birdie them all?"

What makes the Ben Hogan story most incredible is that one

foggy morning in Texas in 1949, when he was at the height of his game, he was nearly killed in a terrible car accident. In a dense fog a Greyhound bus hit the Hogan car head-on. For an hour-and-a-half Ben lay in the wreckage, badly smashed up. Then, he had to endure a 150-mile ride to a hospital in El Paso.

Ben had suffered multiple injuries to his legs and to his hip. It was strongly believed not only would he not play golf again, but that he might not even walk again.

His indomitable will brought him through. Although he was limping badly, he captained the Ryder Cup Team that year in England. Some blood vessels in Hogan's legs had been tied off so that when he walked his legs had that constant feeling of "pins and needles." Although he feared he could not complete the 72 holes required in an Open tournament, he signed up for the Los Angeles Open. All competitors had to walk whether they had injured legs or not and no exception would be made for Ben Hogan.

Ben played anyway and tied for first place, but lost the playoff. A few months later he won the U.S. Open at Merion after tieing with Lloyd Mangrum and George Fazio. A year later he brought "The Monster", the Oakland Hills course at Birmingham, Michigan, to its knees with an unbelievable 69 on his last round.

In 1953 he won the Masters, the U.S. Open at Oakmont, and the British Open at Carnoustie.

In order to acclimate himself to the Scottish golf links and the small 1.64 centimeter ball used in the British Open, Hogan went over to Scotland two weeks ahead of time. He rented a house a few miles away near an old Army firing range. It was said that the casual observer could not tell the difference between the shells being fired on the range and the "bullets" being shot by Hogan.

He analyzed the Carnoustie course hole by hole, walking it backward. At last he was ready to go. The weather was foul—raw and windy. Furthermore, Ben was sick with a heavy cold. He shot 73, 71, 70, and a last round of 68, one of the best he had ever played. He birdied the twelfth hole, a vicious dog-leg par-5 every time he played it, driving a low running shot past a dangerous bunker, and then landing his second shot on the green. Ben won the coveted title by

four strokes over the field. The crowds cheered their "Wee Ice Mon,"
who showed them golf as it should be played.

At last the effect of his injuries caught up with Hogan. He lost his putting touch primarily because he could not get the proper signals of balance from his ravaged legs.

Here is an account of one of Ben's last glorious moments before he finally retired from competition. It was one of the most heart-warming scenes in the history of golf.

It was the third day of the 1967 Masters. Ben was making a token appearance, it was thought. His game was gone. Out in a respectable 36, he gave no sign of the fireworks he intended to show on the second nine.

At the tenth hole he sank a 7-foot putt for a birdie-3. At the eleventh he was one foot from the cup in 2 and had his second birdie in a row. At the short twelfth he put a 6-iron fifteen feet from the cup and made a 2, his third birdie in a row. He reached the par-5 thirteenth hole in 2 strokes and down went the fourth birdie.

He parred the fourteenth and again made the par-5 fifteenth green in 2 and birdied that hole, too. Now he was 5-under par. Pars at the sixteenth and seventeenth holes brought him to the 18th needing a sixth birdie to break the course record.

The eighteenth at Augusta is a long hard walk uphill. Poor Ben's legs were tired. Laboriously, slowly, he made that climb, step by step. His tee shot was good. His second carried the bunker in front of the green and skidded to a stop twenty-five feet above the hole.

As Ben walked those last 160 yards to the green, the gallery came to life. They knew they were seeing a living legend, one of the greatest golfers of all time proving his courage and skill in one last magnificent effort of concentration and perfect execution of the golf swing. The crowd continued its tremendous applause for Ben. He tipped his little white hat and there were tears in his eyes as he was enveloped by the heartfelt, thundering, unending display of admiration.

Of course he rolled that twenty-five-foot putt right into the hole for his sixth birdie and a course record score of 30 strokes. Do you think his guardian angel would have allowed him to miss that last putt?

SAM SNEAD

Sam Snead, a real hillbilly, played his early golf barefooted. He grew up in Hot Springs, Virginia and, as a youth, caddied at the famous Homestead resort golf course. The caddies were allowed to play on Mondays. One day the owner of the Homestead saw Sam drive the ball onto a green more than 300 yards away. From then on, Sam had a sponsor. He gave Sam a job in the Pro Shop and eventually encouraged him to test his golfing skills against other great stars of that time, Ben Hogan and Byron Nelson.

Snead developed a smooth, fluid swing that incorporated a big shoulder turn. "Slammin' Sam" could drive the ball farther than any of the other players of his time with the exception of Jimmy Thomson. When Snead was asked what he did to hit an extra long drive he said, "All I do is make everything move faster."

Although Sam won the Masters three times, the PGA three times, and the British Open once, he never could win the U.S. Open.

In his first U.S. Open at Oakland Hills in Birmingham, Michigan in 1937 Sam came into the tournament a heavy favorite to win. He had been burning up the courses, and Oakland Hills, notoriously long and tough, was well suited to his game. Snead was in the clubhouse with a score of 283 having finished early. He appeared to be the winner. Suddenly he heard a roar from the crowd around the eighth green, 200 yards away. Ralph Guldahl had just sunk a long putt for an eagle-3 that put him in the lead. He would beat Snead if he could par the second nine. Par on the Oakland Hills second nine is extremely difficult to achieve, especially under foot-deep open rough conditions. Guldahl lost a stroke at the tenth hole but got a birdie-2 on the thirteenth. Steady pars and a save from the bunker at the fifteenth brought Guldahl home the winner at 281.

Another terribly disappointing moment in Snead's career came in the 1939 U.S. Open at Philadelphia Country Club. He had only two holes to go, and two pars would give him a total of 282 strokes, which would be two shots ahead of Byron Nelson, Craig Wood, and Denny Shute who each had posted scores of 284. The seventeenth hole is a short easy par-4. Snead hit a good drive followed by a weak second shot to the green. He left his first putt six feet short of the cup, his second a foot shy, and the result was a damaging bogey.

Now all he needed was a bogey-6 on the 558 yard par-5 eighteenth to tie or a par to win the title outright. Sam was very upset with himself over the way he had played the seventeenth hole. But, he looked forward with confidence to the eighteenth hole. In his previous rounds he had been reaching that green easily in two strokes. It was practically a par-4 for him.

Sam was so anxious to hit his tee shot that he brushed aside his playing partner who had the honor, the right to play first. Snead decided to smash a long drive.

Sadly, Sam moved everything too quickly. He hit a duck-hook into the left rough where the gallery had trampled the grass into a matted jungle. In spite of a questionable lie, Snead decided to use his brassie, a wood club without much loft, to get out of the rough and close to the green. He took a mighty swing and smashed the ball into the face of a bunker only a hundred yards ahead. Sad to relate, Sam's next stroke did not get the ball out of the bunker. Snead lay 4 and was not yet on the green.

He hit his fifth shot onto the green. Knowing that he had to sink his long putt in order to tie, he went for it and putted three feet past the hole. Carelessly, he missed that putt, too. He walked away, in a daze. Sam had blown another U.S. Open, an experience he never forgot. Nor was he ever allowed to forget it by the newspapermen or his opponents.

Still haunted by this experience, he came close once more in the 1947 U.S. Open at St. Louis Golf Club. There he had to make a putt of about thirty inches to defeat Lou Worsham. Worsham's ball also lay about thirty inches away. Lou said, "I think I'm away," as Sam stepped up to sink his putt. Sam stepped back, flustered.

The officials measured the putts and determined that Sam was away by a half-inch. Sam putted weakly and pushed the ball to the side of the cup. Worsham made his putt and then won the playoff the next day. Sam never again got as close to winning a U.S. Open.

Sam is notoriously thrifty. Some say he has hundreds of pairs of brand new, never-worn golf shoes in the attic of his house near the Homestead. There are rumors, too, that he has never trusted banks and that all of his money is buried in tin cans in his back yard.

Years ago when Sam took his first train ride, he arrived in New York and was greeted with a newspaper article containing his photograph. Sam asked, "How did they get that? I've never been in New York before in my life!"

There's an interesting story about the way Snead won his second Masters title in 1952. He and Hogan had had a long, continuing rivalry, and in that tournament they completed the third round tied for the lead at 214 strokes apiece.

The two arch rivals went into the final day with the golf world hanging on each stroke. Surely, relentless, machinelike Ben Hogan would beat Sam Snead. Sam would skyrocket again. Hadn't he done it many times before?

Snead was scheduled to start an hour ahead of Hogan. Sam played well for eleven holes and then it appeared that Sam would again blow up. The twelfth hole at Augusta National is a tiny par-3 with a pond in front and on the right side of the green. And there are mean bunkers around its perimeter. The winds, too, are tricky and can blow a golf ball into trouble. Sam dunked his tee shot in the water. He dropped a ball over his shoulder and with the penalty stroke assessed him for going in the water, Sam was shooting his third shot for the green. He still had to cross that dangerous pond.

He swung and almost put the ball in the water again. This time the grass at the edge of the green saved him. But he had a terrible lie. He was playing his fourth shot and looking at the probability of a 6 or worse on the par-3, a loss of three or more strokes of his precious lead.

Sam did his best with a very difficult shot from an awkward stance, one foot higher than the other. He chipped the ball up onto the green, and it rolled and rolled toward the hole, never hesitating at the cup and plunked right in for a sweet bogey-4, one of the best bogeys Sam had ever made in his life. Sam regained his composure, settled down, played the rest of the nine in sound fashion and finished the round with a remarkable 72 under great pressure. At 286 he would beat Ben Hogan provided that Ben did not score 71 or better. Word came that Ben was having putting woes. Five times, Ben Hogan three-putted. He had only a single one-putt that day. The roof had fallen in on "the mechanical man." He finished with a 79, seven over par, when he had needed only a par round to tie. Hogan was not unbeatable that day. Sam Snead was.

Here's a story about another bad hole by Sam Snead. This time it happened in the 1958 Western Open at Plum Hollow Golf Club outside Detroit, Michigan.

The fourth hole at Plum Hollow is a straightaway 445-yard par-4 which runs along 9 Mile Road on its right side. The right rough is only about fifteen yards wide so there is no margin for error on the right, the out-of-bounds side of the hole.

In his second round of the tournament Sam drove his first ball over the fence, out-of-bounds. He teed up another ball, now shooting three, and as he said later, "put it through the same hole in the sky." He was out-of-bounds again and now he was playing his fifth stroke and still was on the tee. This shot found the fairway but his next one, his sixth, went into a bunker on the right side of the green. Then he failed to get out of the bunker on his first attempt. At last he got on the green with his eighth, twenty feet away from the cup. He putted to within three feet and sank his tenth shot. His caddie said later, "He nearly missed the 3-footer, too!"

Sam lost six strokes to the field right there but if he had been able to sink a 6-footer on the 72nd hole on Sunday he would have tied for first place.

Soon afterward the members of Plum Hollow considered his feat noteworthy and placed a bronze plaque on the fourth tee to commemorate the deed. It read, "Duffers take heart! On this, the fourth hole at Plum Hollow on July 14, 1958 Sam Snead took ten strokes. In spite of this horrendous disaster he finished at 283 strokes, only one stroke behind the winner, Doug Ford."

Many of the newspapers and golf magazines carried the story of the "Snead plaque." For a while Snead enjoyed the publicity as golfers from Detroit and around the world would visit the Greenbrier, Sam's home club and tell him, "Sam, I saw your marker the other day at Plum Hollow."

At last he could stand it no longer. The constant reminder of his "horrendous disaster" was getting to him. So he requested, even ordered, Plum Hollow to take it away. "Get that thing out of there!" The marker was removed and today it can be seen in the PGA Golf Museum reminding duffers to "take heart" with the unspoken advice that if Sam Snead can take a ten on a hole, you shouldn't feel too bad if you do, too.

A number of years ago, Snead had such bad putting "yips" that he decided to try putting in croquet style with one hand held high on the shaft of the club and the other down low with the ball positioned between his feet. The style seemed to work better for him than the traditional method which is a miniature golf swing. Then the USGA decided that the new variation was contrary to golf tradition and ruled that the golfer may not straddle the ball when using such a stroke. Sam adapted to the new ruling and now putts in a side-saddle version of the croquet stroke. And he putts extremely well with it.

Sam Snead, one of the greatest golfers of all time and still going strong in his early 70s has won 84 "official" PGA tour victories, more than any other player in history.

MILDRED DIDRIKSON ZAHARIAS

In 1945 Mildred "Babe" Didrikson Zaharias (1913-1956) was named "Woman Athlete of the Year." In 1950 United States sports experts ranked her number one on the list of the greatest female athletes of the first half of the twentieth century. A tomboy in her early years, she went on to star in basketball, baseball, track and field, and finally golf.

In 1932 Babe entered seven events in the National A.A.U. Track and Field championships. She won the javelin throw, the baseball throw, the shot put, the broad jump, the eighty-meter hurdles, and tied for first in the high jump. Now there was a versatile athlete!

Two weeks later in the 1932 Olympics she established a new woman's world record on the javelin. Then she broke the record in the high hurdles. Though tied for first in the high jump, she was disqualified when the judges of that day refused to accept her head-first jump over the bar.

Babe was a great basketball player, too, and once when she missed a foul shot that cost her team the game, she shot 300 fouls a day in practice and atonement for her mistake.

At the urging of sports columnist Grantland Rice, she took up golf. They say that her first drive went over 250 yards down the fairway. Not long afterward, in another round, she was home in two on the 523-yard seventeenth hole at Brentwood Country Club in Santa Monica.

After the Olympics she became a professional golfer and toured the country for a while with Gene Sarazen. Her golf game around the greens was shaky, but she could belt those drives. When she was asked how she did it, she'd say, "I just hitch up my girdle and let 'er fly."

She knew that her short game was weak so she decided to work at

113

becoming a top golfer. To help her attain her goal, the great golf teacher Tommy Armour taught her many of the finer points of the game. Babe worked long hours on the practice tee perfecting her technique. She hit so many balls her hands blistered and broke into raw sores. She bandaged them, soaked them in brine, and went right on practicing. It began to pay off.

About this time she met George Zaharias, a mountain-sized wrestler. It was love at first sight for George and Babe. After they were married, George used to follow her around to the various tournaments admiring his wonderful golfing wife. In those days there was no regular women's golf circuit. A tournament in California might be followed in three weeks by one in Massachusetts, or vice versa.

Once she had strengthened her game, she really attacked golf with a vengeance. Now she wanted to become the best woman golfer in the world. Once again she played in an exhibition match at Brentwood and this time she shot a 65. On another day, with a strong wind behind her, she drove a ball 408 yards.

Babe Didrikson was a professional and of course wanted to play against the best women players. Most of them were in the amateur ranks, so she asked the USGA to allow her to renounce her professional status and become an amateur again. The request was granted in 1944. When World War II was over Babe was ready to play in the U.S. Women's Amateur Championship. Babe won her first two matches by big margins, 4 and 3 each time. Then Maureen Orcutt, a past champion herself, lost to Babe, 6 and 4. Didrikson's semi-final match against Helen Sigel was a little tougher. Babe was nervous and got off to a bad start, but she roared back, winning at the sixteenth hole. In the final she defeated Clara Sherman 11 and 9, the largest margin ever registered in this championship.

Babe went on to win fifteen straight tournaments in 1946 and 1947. She then decided to go after the British Ladies Golf championship, which was to be played on the hilly course at Gullane, Scotland. (The Scots call it "Gillin.")

In the eight rounds she played there she was off the fairway only three times. She visited only three bunkers. On one of those bunker

shots she holed out and on the others she had short putts for "gim-
mies." She won the title in brilliant fashion.

Having proved she was the best woman golfer in the world, she accepted an offer of $300,000 to make some movie shorts and again
turned professional.

In 1953 she found that she had cancer and she underwent radical
surgery for its removal. After the operation she practiced hard to re-
gain her strength and vowed that she would best the disease. Once
more she won the U.S. Open—the third time in her illustrious career.
Her margin of victory was great—twelve strokes over her nearest
competitor.

Sadly, the cancer recurred and Babe succumbed at last to the inev-
itable. She had won more than fifty events—a champion to the end.

JO ANNE CARNER

Just as Babe Didrikson was called the greatest woman golfer of the 1940s, Jo Anne Carner is considered to be the greatest of the modern era. She joined the LPGA, Ladies Professional Golf Association, after an outstanding career as an amateur. Known then as "The Great Gundy" (her maiden name was Gunderson), she won five U.S. Amateur Championship titles, 1957, 1960, 1962, 1966, and 1968 to tie the record of Glenna Collett Vare who also won five times between 1922 and 1935. Jo Anne even achieved the distinction of winning a Ladies PGA Open, the Burdine's Invitational, as an amateur just before she became a professional.

Since becoming a pro, Carner has won more tournaments, thirty-nine, and earned more money ($1.8 million) than any other woman golfer in history. She was named the tenth member of the LPGA Hall of Fame and was the first woman golfer to earn over $200,000 for three consecutive years.

Jo Anne is 5-feet 7-inches tall. She is outgoing, friendly, and even-tempered, always smiling even when the putts don't go down. She is famous for her short swing that propels the golf ball prodigious distances. It has been said that if all the LPGA tournaments were played on long golf courses Carner might win every time. As it is, with many of the courses shortened to 6,000-yard length, Jo Anne must often play irons from many tees for fear of driving through the fairway.

She is known for the gyrations of her body when she misses a putt and the anguish she conveys in her expressive face.

When Jo Anne Carner came on the tour in 1970 everyone expected her to win immediately, but she started off in a horrible slump. In her first year as a pro she earned a mere $14,000. It was not until 1974, when she earned $87,000, that she truly hit her stride and worked out the problems with her swing. She put herself under

117

the tutelage of Gardner Dickinson, a protegé himself of Ben Hogan. He discovered that Jo Anne was making an improper weight shift and after much practice Jo Anne got it right.

Jo Anne credits the fiery baseball manager Billy Martin for giving her career a great psychological boost just when she needed it.

They met in Florida in 1974 when Billy watched Jo Anne in a couple of early tournaments. After seeing her play, Billy gave Jo Anne a serious lecture that went something like this:

"What are you doing out there? With such a big game why are you just patty-caking it around the golf course? Do you think something lucky is going to happen? You used to make things happen. You used to charge, you used to be very positive and now you're afraid of scoring an 80. Hell, the next day you can score 66 and you are one of the few who are capable of making that kind of a score."

"With his advice ringing in my ears, I decided that Billy was right—I had been playing too cautiously so I stopped patty-caking it around the course and started 'letting 'er fly.' I didn't care where the ball came down. I knew it would hit the ground somewhere. Suddenly I found that the ball was coming down on the fairway and frequently right on the flagstick. It was like recovering from an illness. I could play aggressive golf again—and I did."

Jo Anne also went on a strict diet and managed to lose twenty-two unwanted pounds that seemed to get in the way of her smooth swinging.

She said, "Losing that weight gave me extra stamina especially when I have to play extra holes on a hot humid day on a long demanding course."

In 1979 Jo Anne suffered a serious injury to her wrist when, on a mountain trail, she lost control of her motorbike on loose gravel. Her injury, though severe, might have ended her career but it did not. She stayed off the tour for a few months healing her wounds but came back to play while she was still hurting. The accident probably cost her $100,000 in lost earnings in 1979 for she jumped from $98,000 that year to $185,000 in 1980 and then had the three straight years over $200,000.

Alice Dye, wife of Pete Dye, the excellent golf course designer, re-

lates the story about the way Jo Anne Carner attacks the golf course **119**
and her opponent in a golf match. Alice, herself a fine golfer, was
playing Jo Anne a head-to-head match on a western course that featured some mean-looking cactus plants. Alice said, "I was in the fairway with an easy shot to the green. Jo Anne had hit the ball into a
cactus and I knew there was no way she could get out of it without
taking a penalty stroke. I could see her looking the shot over carefully. Then she asked her caddie for her rain-suit. She put on the
pants, backed her rear end into the cactus, and while being stabbed
by the cactus needles, she played a long iron out of the trouble and
put her ball on the green. I couldn't believe it. It was a miraculous
shot."

Another time as Jo Anne was about to win a tournament in Or-
lando, Florida, she hit an errant drive. Her line to the par-5 green was
over trees and a big lake, a 240-yard carry. She asked the marshals
to clear the gallery from the right side of the fairway and boomed a
3-wood over the trees, over the water onto the green and won the
tournament.

Jo Anne and her husband, Don, traveled from tournament to tournament early in her golfing career towing a small trailer behind their
car. They lived in the trailer when they came back to home base,
Lake Worth, Florida. Jo Anne and Don now travel in a quarter-of-a-
million dollar motor home with every possible convenience. They
live in a condominium in Palm Beach overlooking the Atlantic
ocean when they are not traveling to another tournament. They also
have recently bought a sea-going yacht and since both Don and Jo
Anne are avid fishermen they are spending more and more time
hunting fish rather than Dunlop golf balls.

When Jo Anne was asked recently if she had any intention of giving up the grind of professional golf she said, "I love the game. I love
the competition and as long as I can play it I will. It would be nice,
though, just to play friendly golf some day."

ARNOLD PALMER

There seems to be a natural law that periodically in sports games a master will arise and set standards of achievement higher than ever before. Such a leader was Arnold Palmer, the symbol of modern professional golf and without doubt the acknowledged hero of the golfing world.

The game of golf underwent a tremendous boom in the late 1950s and early 1960s and a great deal of the credit for the increased public interest in the game must go to Palmer. After winning the U.S. Amateur championship in 1954, Palmer promptly turned professional and soon afterward won the Canadian Open for the first of his 61 victories. He won the Masters every other year from 1958 to 1964, the U.S. Open in 1960, the British Open in 1961 and 1962, and played on six Ryder Cup teams.

One of the most dramatic comebacks in Arnold's career happened in the 1960 U.S. Open at Cherry Hills in Denver, Colorado. The air there, a mile above sea level, is thin, so Arnold was able to drive the ball great distances. In this tournament he played the first three rounds in 72, 71, and 72. Par was 71 so he was two-over par as he started his last round. Mike Souchak was leading the field and was seven shots in front of Arnold, 208 to 215.

Young Jack Nicklaus, then an amateur, was four strokes ahead of Palmer and only three behind Souchak. Arnold told Bob Drum, well-known golf writer, "I may shoot 65 this afternoon. What will that do for me?" Drum told him, "Nothing, you're too far behind."

The first hole at Cherry Hills was a straightaway par-4, 346 yards long. (Since then it has been lengthened and turned into a dogleg.) Arnold, determined to catch Mike Souchak, smashed his drive 340 yards to the center of the first green and two-putted for his birdie. Then he birdied the second hole, a 410-yard par-4, holing a little run-up shot. His third birdie came at the third hole with a wedge second shot one foot from the cup. On the fourth hole Arnold put his wedge eighteen feet from the hole and sank the putt for another birdie. He got a birdie-2 at the sixth and with another wedge stiff to the flag on the seventh hole, he had his sixth birdie in seven holes.

Arnold was out in 30 strokes and had grabbed the lead as the other contenders either fell back or failed to match his incredible burst of great golf. He played the second nine in 35 with eight pars and one birdie. His 65 was the lowest round ever scored by the winner of an Open until Johnny Miller shot 63 on his last round at Oakmont in 1973.

The term "an Arnold Palmer charge" had been born and would follow him through his long illustrious career.

Palmer is known for his daring style of play. No lie is too tough for him, no flagstick so well-guarded that he has to play safe in attacking it. He gave everything he had, or so it seemed, to every shot. His putting touch at the height of his success was nothing less than magical. With a peculiar knock-kneed stance that locked his body into a firm platform, it seemed that Arnie could and did will the ball to the cup.

One of the most famous sport pictures of the 1950s is that of Arnold hurling his visored cap high into the air in a joyous salute to another victory.

No one else, either, ever seemed to be more anguished over a missed putt than Arnie. His personality was so attractive to the crowds of golf fans that soon after he started his remarkably successful career he drew hordes of shoving, pushing fans who adopted him as their own. The crowds came to be called "Arnie's Army" and of course, Arnie himself became known as "The General." Palmer's progress around the courses could easily be tracked by the decibel pitch of the crowds reacting as he sank putts for birdies, eagles, or even for routine pars.

The crowds around the greens often acted as barriers to any Palmer ball that might go too far astray. It was even said that occasionally a Palmer ball would be thrown back onto a green for Arnie. When Jack Nicklaus first came out to challenge Arnie's right as number one, the crowds resented Jack and called him names such

as "Fat Jack" or would even applaud a bad shot by Nicklaus. Eventually the crowds accepted Jack for the great golfer and good sports-
man he truly is, but in the early days of their competition, a pairing
of Nicklaus and Palmer was an explosive one for crowd control.

Arnold has a great sense of humor and does not take himself too
seriously. Perhaps that is part of his great appeal to his followers. In
the 1961 Masters Gary Player led Palmer by four strokes on the last
day of the tournament. Player fell off badly on his last nine to take 40
strokes and was in the clubhouse with a 280. Palmer came to the
eighteenth hole after making what appeared to be a true Palmer
charge at the lead. Arnie needed only a par-4 to win, a bogey to tie
Player.

Arnie drove well to the center of the fairway. Then he put his second shot into the right bunker. The lie was a nasty one, downhill and
sidehill. All he had to do now was blast the ball out and two-putt for a
tie. Instead, he skimmed the ball over the green down an embank-
ment on the left. He could still have saved his tie with Player with a
delicate run-up shot. He elected to putt up the slope. He putted badly
and ran the ball twenty feet beyond the hole. He took two more putts
and Gary had backed into his first Masters title.

Palmer smiled and said, "I remember thinking before I hit that second shot all I have to do is get it on the green and two-putt for a four.
That's where I made my mistake, thinking about something besides
the ball. If I'd just kept my mind on swinging the club properly, there
wouldn't have been any problem."

In the 1966 U.S. Open at Olympic Country Club at San Francisco
Palmer led Billy Casper by three strokes, 207 to 210 as they both
started the last round playing together. Casper was wild off the tee
on the first nine as Palmer blistered the first nine holes in 32 strokes,
three under par. Arnie then led Casper by seven strokes with only
nine holes to go.

At the tenth Palmer took three strokes from the edge of the green.
He hit a bad iron shot at the thirteenth and another stroke was gone.
With five holes to play he still led by five strokes. Then he lost two at
the short 150-yard, par-3 fifteenth, taking a four while Casper sank a
twenty-footer for a birdie-2.

The sixteenth hole was a par-5, 604 yards long. Arnold hooked his drive into the trees and mucked an iron shot trying to extricate himself from trouble. Then he landed in a bunker. Casper was on his way to a cool birdie-4—Arnold 6, Casper 4, and the lead was down to one stroke.

Arnold drove badly again at the seventeenth and failed to sink a five-and-a-half foot putt for par. The match was tied. Both players parred the last hole, Arnold just managing to sink a tricky four-footer. In the playoff the next day Casper beat Palmer soundly 69 to 73. Casper had accomplished an unbelievable come-from-behind victory in the U.S. Open—a "reverse charge" against the famous Arnold Palmer.

On another occasion Palmer was playing the eighteenth hole in the 1967 Los Angeles Open at the Rancho Park Golf Course in Los Angeles. His score was near the top of the field as he drove into the fairway on the short par-5 hole. On the right side of the hole extending from the clubhouse out about 240 yards is a fenced-in driving range. It is protected by a chain-link fence about thirty feet high. On the left hand side is Patricia Avenue close to the fairway which narrows to a bottleneck at the green.

Palmer hit his second shot into the range, dropped another ball, penalty stroke, hitting four. His next shot went out of bounds onto Patricia Avenue. Another ball, another penalty stroke! Bang! Into the range again. Then, one more shot onto Patricia Avenue. At last, on his tenth shot Arnold was on the green. He made a twelve. Someone asked him how he did it. He laughed and said, "If I hadn't sunk a good-sized putt I would have had thirteen."

Arnold Palmer was not only "The General" but undoubtedly the King and probably the most exciting player of modern-day golf.

JACK NICKLAUS

Jack Nicklaus was winner of the United States Athlete of the Decade (1970-1979) Award. This is awarded to the best athlete in all American sports over a ten-year period. That practically says it all.

Jack's record is unmatched in golf history. He has won seventy tour victories and finished second or third ninety-one times. Eight times between 1964 and 1976 he had the lowest scoring average. He has been named PGA Player of the Year five times.

When he was a youth in the early 1950s, Jack's father, a well-to-do pharmacist in Columbus, Ohio, encouraged Jack to persevere with golf. He even built a special golf driving net in the basement of the Nicklaus residence. To do that, it was necessary to excavate an extra two feet to give Jack swinging room. The Nicklauses were members of a magnificent golf course in Columbus, Scioto Country Club, designed by the world-famous golf architect, Donald Ross, a Scot who specialized in building deep, forbidding sand bunkers, and small, undulating greens.

In the wintertime at Scioto a special Quonset hut open at one end enabled the young Nicklaus to drive his five-hundred practice golf balls a day. Jack's father and his professional teacher, Jack Grout, felt that Jack should learn to hit the ball hard. "Later on, we'll teach him to hit it straight." Jack's game prospered and soon he was driving the ball prodigious distances. At the age of thirteen, Jack won the Ohio State Junior Championship. More remarkable, playing against a field of professionals at the age of sixteen, he won the Ohio State Open. His final rounds were 64 and 72—a sixteen year old!

No wonder the world of golf started to take notice of the young man from the Buckeye State.

At nineteen he won his first major championship, the U.S. Amateur, defeating Charlie Coe who had, himself, won the title twice before in 1949 and 1958. By this time Jack had grown to 5-feet 11-inches, and had developed an unusually strong body and tremendously powerful legs. That enabled him to drive the ball high and extremely far, which meant he had to temper his stroke in the 1961 U.S. Amateur championship held at Pebble Beach, California. There is a chasm on the right-hand side of the eighth hole at Pebble Beach some 285 yards from the tee. Jack found that he had to "lay up" there with a 1-iron because he was hitting his 3-wood over the edge of the cliff. Jack defeated Dudley Wysong 8 and 6 in the final match to win his second amateur title.

At last at the age of twenty-two, Jack decided to become a professional golfer. The lure of the money on the professional tour was proving too great. He left Ohio State University just a few course credits short of getting his degree in business administration. It was there that he got his nickname "The Bear," because he looks somewhat like a bear. Later, on the tour, with his sun-bleached hair, he became "The Golden Bear."

In his first pro tournament he won only $33.33—a disappointing start. Five months later he won his first major tournament, the 1962 U.S. Open, when he defeated Arnold Palmer at Oakmont, Pennsylvania, in a playoff, 71 to 74. He would go on to win nineteen major championships (five Masters, five PGA championships, four U.S. Opens, and three British Opens in addition to the two U.S. Amateur championships he had already won).

In 1965 he took the Augusta National Golf Course apart with a third-round course record score of 64. This enabled him to beat the field by a whopping nine strokes (271 to the 280 scores of Arnold Palmer and Gary Player). Jack had nineteen birdies in the four days, eight of them on his record round. He exhibited his awesome power by using no more than a drive and 6-iron to any par-4 green and he reached the par-5s (the second, eighth, thirteenth, and fifteenth holes) in two strokes each with drives and 3-irons or 5-irons. The eighth hole is 520 yards long. The Golden Bear covered the ground with a drive and a 5-iron that momentous day.

Reminiscing about that round Jack talked about the part pure luck sometimes plays. He was one under par when he reached the 220-yard long par-3 fourth hole. That day the tee was placed between the

back and front tee so it played about 195 yards into the wind. Jack said, "I hit my four-iron 'fat' [meaning behind the ball] and was disgusted with the shot. A photographer took my picture when I made a terrible face. My shot just barely carried the front bunker, hit, and rolled to about ten feet away from the hole. I made the two for another birdie. The putt had a left to right bend."

The film of the 1965 Masters shows, too, that Jack nearly three-putted the thirteenth hole that year. After making the green 455 yards away in two shots with a drive and a 5-iron, his first putt from forty-five feet away from the cup left him eight feet short. He had a slippery downhill, sidehill putt to make. His putt just barely reached the front edge of the cup, hesitated a moment, and then toppled in. Again, Lady Luck was with him.

Another tremendously dramatic Nicklaus victory occurred in 1970 at the Old Course in St. Andrews, Scotland, when Doug Sanders needed only to sink a three-and-a-half-foot putt on the eighteenth green to beat Jack by one stroke. Here's what happened:

One stroke ahead of Jack Nicklaus at the seventy-second tee, Doug Sanders could win the historic British Open championship if he scored a par-4 on the last hole, the eighteenth, with its monstrous green and its forbidding entrance through the treacherous Valley of Sin.

Doug drove carefully and placed his shot to the left, away from the out-of-bounds on the right. He then had to make a pitch-shot of seventy yards to the plateaued green.

His pitch-shot rolled on and on, past the hole, into a very dangerous position above it. The green was very slick. Doug Sanders needed to get down in two strokes to win. The slope was a little to his right and he overestimated the effect it would have on the ball and left himself with a second putt of three-and-a-half feet.

Doug stood up to the putt and then stepped away to pick up what he later said was a pebble near or on his line to the cup. He seemed to have lost his concentration. Sanders then pushed the putt to the right. The ball never touched the hole. Five strokes, a bogey, on the eighteenth, cost sentimental favorite Doug Sanders the outright title and threw him into a tie with formidable Jack Nicklaus.

The next day Nicklaus beat Sanders in the playoff, 72 to 73 for his first British Open championship.

Another highlight of Jack's career happened in the 1975 Masters.

Tom Weiskopf had taken the lead at the end of the third round and the scoreboard looked like this:

| Weiskopf | 69 | 72 | 66 | 207 |
| Nicklaus | 68 | 67 | 73 | 208 |

That day Nicklaus was playing in the twosome immediately ahead of Weiskopf and Miller. Weiskopf had lost his lead when he dunked his tee-shot into the pond in front of the eleventh green, giving Nicklaus the edge. After Jack three-putted the fourteenth, Tom followed with a birdie-3 to seize the lead once more.

Nicklaus was one stroke behind Weiskopf as he reached the 190-yard sixteenth, the "water-hole," famous to television audiences all over the world because of the breath-taking beauty of its blue lake surrounded by azaleas and dogwood. Nicklaus' tee shot found the green safely, but he faced a nasty forty-foot left-to-right breaking putt.

The cup on the sixteenth hole was cut that day on the far right top corner of the green, in a most awkward place. Jack later said that he "knew he could make the putt" because some years before from the same spot he had had the same putt and had holed it. He struck the putt firmly and "knew" it would be good. He started to dance to his right with his putter raised in the air as the ball made its last necessary veer for the center of the hole. Down it went for the birdie-2. The customarily reticent Nicklaus leaped into the air in elation.

Jack's birdie and the resultant roars of the massed crowd must have affected Tom Weiskopf who was waiting on the sixteenth tee. He had memories of other tee-shots into the water on the left, and, overly cautious, hit a weak iron to the front of the sixteenth green, never really having a chance for his par. He left his first putt woefully short of the cup, eighteen feet away. Jack was once more in the lead and he never lost it, winning by that single stroke over Weiskopf.

Jack Nicklaus, a strong family man, now limits his professional appearances to about fifteen of the most important world tournaments. That way he can spend more time at home, fishing, playing tennis, and cheering his sons on in their own athletic careers. Jack and Barbara Nicklaus have four sons, Jack Jr., Steve, Michael, and Gary (named for Gary Player) and a daughter Nancy. Already Jack, Jr. and Gary are showing great promise as golfers. Young Gary, in a driving contest last year, managed to hit his ball 340 yards. Perhaps one day another Nicklaus may surpass the records of Jack William Nicklaus?

Considered by many the greatest golfer in the history of the game, Jack Nicklaus was named "Golfer of the Century" in 1988. In 1997, Jack played his 10,000th hole in a major championship. In his successful career, it is estimated that Jack has walked 9,620 miles on various golf courses, figuring them at 7,000 yards or nearly four miles per course.

Through 1997, Jack had taken 170,061 strokes during 2,405 rounds as a professional golfer. Jack has earned $7,964,696 in official PGA tour money. Not counted is $221,366 earned on the Senior Tour. He won his 100th professional victory when he captured The Tradition in 1996 for the fourth time.

As a golf course designer, Jack has now designed more than sixty golf courses all over the world at a reported fee of $1,000,000 per course.

TOM WATSON

Tom Watson is only 5-feet 9-inches tall and weighs 160 pounds. He is one of the greatest golfers in the world and one of the few golfers in the modern age who can drive the ball 300 yards or more.

Tom was born in Kansas Ciy in 1949. His father was his early teacher in golf. Although Tom played college golf for Stanford University he really did not show exceptional promise then. He decided to play professional golf in 1971. In his first start as a pro he finished twenty-eighth and won $1,065 for his efforts. Since then his record has been amazing.

Watson has won 31 PGA tournaments in the United States as well as five British Open Championships. He has won a total of $3,580,163 (not counting the British titles) and in 1980 was the first player to win more than a half-million dollars in one year. He just barely missed doing it again in 1984 with $476,000.

Tom has been named PGA player of the year no less than six times—1977, 1978, 1979, 1980, 1982, and 1984.

It has been said that Watson came onto the golf scene and challenged the reign of Jack Nicklaus and has successfully toppled Jack from his throne. But both golfers are champions and remarkable athletes.

One of Tom's first important victories was the Masters of 1977. In 1976 and early 1977 Tom had appeared to falter several times when he had a chance to win a major title. He would "blow up" on his last round and someone else would waltz in with a good score and seize the victory. In the 1977 Masters, Watson finally overcame this tendency and won his first major title.

On the last day of that tournament, "the Bear", Jack Nicklaus was playing directly in front of Watson. Nicklaus was making great shots as he often does on the last round of a tournament. He birdied six of

132   the first thirteen holes. Watson matched him stroke for stroke and returned a 67 for Nicklaus's 66 to win by two strokes, 276 to 278.

Here is how he did it: Nicklaus had started the day at 212 strokes, three behind Watson, and by the 10th hole Jack had narrowed the gap to two strokes.

Watson began his round at 7-under par and held that red figure as he parred the first four holes. Then he rammed in birdies on the next four holes, the fifth through the eighth. Watson had gained four strokes on par by then and stood at 11-under par after eight holes.

Jack Nicklaus, playing in the twosome ahead of Watson, started at 4-under par and promptly birdied the first two holes to go 6-under par.

Jack got home in 2 on the uphill eighth and finally cashed a birdie there. That put Nicklaus at 7-under par, 4 strokes behind Watson.

The race narrowed minutes later when Nicklaus was able to birdie the tenth just before Watson's bogey-5 there—Nicklaus 8-under, Watson slipping back to 10-under, only two shots ahead.

Jack's confidence was high as he played the nasty little 3-par water hole, the twelfth. He clicked a sweet 7-iron straight at the flag. His ball ended in a nice flat place on the green and moments later it was in the center of the cup for a birdie-2. That moved Jack to within a single shot of Watson, who had watched the birdie stroke from the twelfth tee, where he was waiting to play his next shot.

Nicklaus got his birdie-4 at the thirteenth hole and momentarily was tied for the lead with Watson at 10-under par. Tom was on the thirteenth comfortably in 2, came close to the eagle-3 that really would have set him up in front, but, most importantly, had gone one stroke ahead of Jack again—Watson 11-under par, Nicklaus 10-under.

Then, what did Watson do but three-putt the fourteenth and once more fall back into a tie with Jack at 10-under.

Nicklaus was heading down the fifteenth, the pond-guarded 5-par. After two prodigious shots, a drive and a towering 4-iron to the back edge of the green, the roar of the crowd and the nearby scoreboard told Nicklaus that Watson had lost his precious lead stroke at the fourteenth.

Watson did not weaken. He came right back with his own birdie at the fifteenth—on the green in two strokes and two putts for the 4. Watson and Nicklaus were again tied, at 11 under par.

Both players got their 3s at the sixteenth. Jack had to tackle the seventeenth hole first. He played it beautifully with a long drive to the left center of the fairway and a marvelously controlled 8-iron to twenty feet from the flag. The putt would not drop. Jack headed for the last hole as Watson's second shot at the seventeenth landed on the green about the same distance away from the hole as Jack's had moments before.

The green was icy, the putt was "impossible" to make. But Watson putted that ball into the center of the cup and did a delighted "war dance" when it went in. Watson was now a stroke ahead with one hole to play.

Nicklaus was on the eighteenth fairway when he heard the cheers from Watson's gallery at the seventeenth hole. He had to get his own birdie or lose out. Jack played a poor shot, caught the bunker in front of the green, and although he blasted out well to only twelve feet from the cup, he did not hole the putt to save his par.

With a two-stroke lead now, Watson played a "safe" par, a 3-wood to the center of the fairway and a 7-iron to twenty feet from the hole. He two-putted and had a two-stroke winning margin in the 41st Masters. Watson had decisively beaten Jack Nicklaus in a head-to-head confrontation down the stretch in a major championship.

Another great victory for Watson came in the 1982 U.S. Open at the famed Pebble Beach links in Carmel, California. Watson's win at Pebble Beach must be viewed against the background of Jack Nicklaus's earlier experiences there.

Jack had won one of the U.S. Amateur titles at Pebble Beach in 1961 before he became a professional and also had won the Bing Crosby Invitational there in 1967 and 1972. The final round of the Crosby is always played at Pebble Beach. It might well be considered to be Jack Nicklaus's home course for he seems to know every blade of grass on it. Tom had played the course many times when he was in college at Stanford but could not be considered as knowledgeable about the links as Jack.

On the final day of play of the U.S. Open at Pebble Beach in 1982, Watson had played himself into the lead with scores of 72, 72, and 68 for 212, to stand three strokes ahead of Nicklaus who was at 215 on scores of 74, 70, and 71. So Jack needed to pick up three strokes on Watson, four to beat him. Nicklaus started his last round slowly with a bogey and a par but sank a long putt on the third for a birdie-3. Then he dropped a 20-footer on the fourth for another birdie. On the fifth he was only two feet from the hole for another birdie. The sixth, a par-5, he reached in two strokes and two-putted for another birdie. On the seventh, the 110-yard par-3, he was only eleven feet from the hole and he canned his fifth birdie in a row. He was now tied with Watson who was playing several holes behind him. Ominously on the seventh hole, Watson missed a 2½-foot putt for a birdie and remained at 4-under par where he stood when he started the round.

An important turning point for Watson happened at the tenth hole, a 424-yard par-4 on the cliffside with the ocean on the right. Watson's second shot found a bunker on the right hand side of the green and he barely avoided sending his ball down the cliff. He exploded to twenty-five feet from the cup and then sank the putt for his par. This putt boosted Watson into the lead because Nicklaus had just three-putted the eleventh hole.

At the eleventh Tom sank a difficult sidehill putt for another birdie and now led Nicklaus by two strokes. Then Watson gave back a stroke with a weak 4 at the 204-yard par-3 twelfth where he bunkered his tee shot, then came out fifteen feet short of the cup, and failed to drop the par-saving putt.

As Watson prepared to putt a 35-footer for a birdie on the fourteenth, a tremendous roar went up from the crowd ahead. The scoreboard nearby soon showed a red "4" for Jack. Jack had birdied the fifteenth hole and was now tied with Tom for the lead. Coolly, Tom putted that difficult downhill, sidehill putt squarely into the back of the hole. Tom again was one stroke ahead.

Tom parred the par-4 fifteenth. He was on the green in two and down in two more from twenty feet. But on the par-4 sixteenth that slides downhill to the right, Tom made a driving error and put himself into a deep pit bunker. All he could do was get the ball out sideways onto the fairway with no thought of making the green. He had to settle for a bogey-5 and with two holes to go he was again tied with Nicklaus.

Now Nicklaus was in the clubhouse at 4-under-par 282. Watson was playing the difficult 209-yard par-3 seventeenth into a strong wind. Tom needed two pars on what are considered by the experts to be two of the most difficult holes in the world. One slip and Nicklaus had the title.

The cup on the seventeenth hole that day was cut well to the left of the wide but short from front-to-back green. Watson played boldly for the flag. His ball drew slightly left and ended on the high rough near the left edge of the green.

At this moment the TV sports announcer with Jack Nicklaus back of the eighteenth green practically conceded the tournament to Nicklaus. He thought Watson could never in a million years make par from the lie he had at seventeen. Furthermore the green sloped away from him steeply. He could conceivably lose another stroke there if the ball "got away" from him.

Tom studied the shot carefully and thinking to himself, "I've practiced this shot a thousand times," took his sand wedge and popped that ball out of the rough safely onto the green above the cup. He could see that the ball was rolling toward the hole so, anticipating that it might go in, Tom started a little dance of victory. Bang, the ball hit the flagstick still traveling fast, and down it went for a miraculous birdie-2. Watson was in the lead by one stroke again.

Tom played the oceanside eighteenth in regulation style, driving safely to the right, laid up short in two and pitched to the green about twenty feet above the cup in three strokes. He did not have to make the last birdie but he did. He was U.S. Open Champion of 1982 and once again he had slammed the door in Jack Nicklaus's face.

Fortunately, a sports photographer was there at the seventeenth green and captured the drama of Tom Watson's "impossible" pitch into the cup for what proved to be the winning margin of victory. More than 100,000 copies of that photo sequence have been sold. It will go down in the history of golf as one of the greatest strokes ever made under pressure.

CALVIN PEETE

Can you imagine a black man who never touched a golf club until he was 23, learning the game then and going on to win more than a million dollars in eight years on the professional tour? Then imagine that the man has a stiff, bent and crippled right elbow from a childhood injury. Fiction? No, fact! This incredible success story belongs to Calvin Peete who has a most unimposing physique and an awkward swing to match. All Peete does is drive the ball so straight down the fairway to the hole that he led all his competition on the PGA tour in accuracy. In 1984 he won the Vardon Trophy for the lowest scoring average of all, 70.56 strokes per round.

Calvin Peete came from a large and poor family. He has eighteen brothers and sisters. In his teens he worked on a farm in Florida and then dropped out of school. As with other black families, Peete said, "Most of us kids had to get jobs as soon as we were old enough to work so we could help out with the expenses." He made a buck by selling wigs, watches and jewelry to migrant workers. He would load his station wagon and follow the transient workers from farm to farm where fruit was being picked. Once, in Rochester, New York, some of his friends invited him to play golf with them.

Calvin Peete had always considered the game a silly one but he gave it a shot and he was hooked. At about the same time he happened to see Jack Nicklaus on television and had heard the announcer say that Jack had won $200,000 chasing the golf ball that year.

Calvin decided he would be happy with one-third that amount so he set about learning how to achieve that goal. With practice his game improved rapidly to the point where he decided to try to play on the professional tour.

But first he had to pass the test of a professional golf tour qualify-

137

ing school. Peete failed. Once more he tried. Again he failed. On his third try he made it and got his playing card.

Calvin had three slim years in 1976, 1977, and 1978 with earnings in the $20,000 range, hardly enough to pay his travel expenses and keep body and soul together, much less support his wife and four children. He was discouraged but he continued on the tour.

At last his game clicked.

In the next six years Calvin won ten tournaments and more than $1,500,000 in prize money. In 1984 he was the best of all in scoring average, in driving accuracy, and finished second in the category called "hitting greens in regulation." That means getting on a par-3 green with his first stroke, on a par-4 green with his second, and on a par-5 green with his third stroke. The closest he came to winning his first major championship was when he finished fourth in the 1984 PGA at Shoal Creek in Alabama, losing to Lee Trevino.

Peete is quiet and self-effacing. He is no "personality kid" by any means. In spite of his impaired right arm he is "sneaky long" with his drives and deadly accurate with his irons. He is not a great putter, but is a good one. If he were a great putter, he would have won a number of other tournaments in which he finished close to the leader.

Calvin Peete takes a business-like approach to his game. He stays away from the party crowd and only occasionally relaxes with a beer.

He explains his seriousness this way, "Since I came from such a large family where it was hard to make ends meet, it was natural that I would adopt a serious attitude about whatever I did whether it was golf or just ordinary life itself. It has paid off for me, too."

Calvin has transformed himself into what amounts to a golfing machine. He has set up a constantly repeating pre-shot routine that practically puts him on "automatic" from the time he selects his club until he releases the club through the ball with a grooved swing that puts the ball down the fairway more frequently that any other golfer on the PGA tour.

The next time Calvin Peete is "on camera" in a televised golf event observe the way he stands directly behind the ball before he makes his shot. He is carefully taking aim and, in his mind, is squaring his

body along that intended line to the green or flagstick. Then he takes exactly two steps forward from behind the ball as he holds his club in his right hand, flexing it a little to keep his hands relaxed.

He steps into his final stance, squares his right foot to the target line, completes his grip, waggles the club a couple of more times, and then fires an extremely straight shot.

Calvin has an interesting style, too, when he wants to curve the ball to the right in a slice, or curve it to the left in a hook. He cocks his head to the right for a slice, to the left for a hook. The next time you watch him, note how he turns his head and you will know in advance the kind of shot he is going to play.

An example of the studiousness of Calvin Peete can be seen in his putting and in his bunker play, both phases of the game that are of utmost importance in saving a par or making a birdie.

At first he was weak in both departments but now, after hundreds of hours of hard practice, he can be considered one of the best in both putting and bunker play.

In his early career as a salesman before he took up golf Calvin had two diamonds of about half-carat size in his front teeth. He said later that he did that to set himself apart from the other peddlers who were selling to the migrant market as well.

When Calvin came out on the PGA tour, he kept his unusually bright smile so the diamonds brought him a certain amount of publicity that ordinarily would not have come to a golfer with a conservative game such as his. When he started to make it big, the diamonds came out. Now Calvin flashes only a very white smile in his very dark face. His excellent golf and remarkable record provide all the sparkle he needs.

Calvin Peete, one of the most successful of today's tournament professionals, once said:

"Starting out in golf, I often thought it would be nice to belong to a country club. Now I just might get to own one."

LAURA DAVIES

Laura Davies was born October 5, 1963 in Coventry, England, about 80 miles northwest of London. She is not married and lives with her mother and stepfather. Her name, incidentally, is pronounced "Davis" in England.

Jo Anne Carner, at 5-feet-7 inches and of varying but substantial weight was nicknamed "Big Mama" Carner. Now that Laura Davies is a star on the LPGA Tour she has inherited a derivation of the nickname and is called "Bigger Mama" Davies. Laura is 5 feet-10-inches tall and her weight fluctuates between 150 pounds and 225 pounds, most of the time near the latter figure.

Laura had a notable record as an amateur golfer in Great Britain. When she was twenty years old she won the English Intermediate Championship and two other prestigious titles. She was a member of the Great Britain and Ireland Curtis Cup Team in 1984.

Laura came over to the United States in 1987 to play and win the 1987 U.S. Women's Open at Plainfield Country Club in Plainfield, New Jersey.

She had tied for first place in the tournament at 285, 3-under par, with Jo Anne Carner and the Japanese golf star, Ayako Okomoto. Laura won the playoff easily with a 71 to Carner's 74 and Ayakamoto's 73.

As a result of this remarkable achievement the LPGA amended its rules to allow Laura admittance to membership without requiring her to attend the Tour's qualifying school.

In 1988, as a rookie, she won two LPGA tournaments and $160,000 in prize money. Since that time she has gone on to a most successful career.

Her best performance came in 1994 when she won three times, including the LPGA championship. She holds the unusual record of having won the same tournament, the Standard Register Ping Tournament, four times in a row. Only Gene Sarazen and Walter Hagen, Hall-of-Famers, had accomplished that unusual feat before Laura did it.

In 1996 Laura played in twenty events and became only the second player to earn more than $900,000 in a single season.

In 1997 she won two more times, her thirteenth and fourteenth LPGA titles and amassed $483,571 in earnings. She has also won thirty-five times overseas in international competition.

In 1996 she recorded a new career low-scoring average of 70.32. She had 23 rounds in the 60s that year. That was the low scoring average for the LPGA Tour but because Laura had played only 63 rounds she was denied the Vare Trophy. She was just short of the 70 rounds requirement to be eligible for the trophy.

Laura is undoubtedly the longest driver of the golf ball who has ever played the LPGA, possibly the longest driver of all time in womens' golf.

The ladies' courses are so short that Laura uses her driver infrequently so as not to have her ball run through the fairway.

The longest drive of her career was struck in Hawaii in 1988. It measured 351 yards. Laura can hit a 2-iron 235 to 240 yards. In 1994 when she won the Sara Lee Classic she dared to take a 2-iron from a bunker 219 yards away from the green. She was able to loft the ball safely out of the bunker and carry the water in front of the green. She made a clutch birdie that enabled her to win the tournament.

Laura makes an average of eight trips a year between her home in England and the United States.

Laura says that she spends $10,000 a year on her clothing. One time she wore some three-year old trousers when she played as a rookie on the European Tour. The Executive Director of the Tour fined her $80 for what he called "unbecoming conduct." Laura never forgot it and never forgave him!

144   She enjoys all kinds of sports, including soccer. She has been known to play on mens' soccer teams and holds her own against strong male soccer players.

Laura drives a $120,000 BMW. At one time early in her career she put a picture of that car on her blackboard and said to herself, "God, I'd love to own one of those cars." Now she does.

Laura has twelve television sets in her home in West Byfleet, England. She has a collection of more than one hundred Teddy bears.

In her recreation room she has a dartboard, a snooker table, and a ping-pong table. In her courtyard she has a basketball backboard and hoop, a tennis court, a swimming pool and nearby, a soccer field. She is truly an all-around athlete.

Queen Elizabeth named Laura a member of the Order of the British Empire in recognition of her marvelous golf record, her sportsmanship and her good character. The M.B.E. award is one of the highest honors that can be bestowed on an English citizen.

Long live Laura Davies. May she continue to bring golfing glory to the British Empire.

ANNIKA SORENSTAM

Annika Sorenstam was born in Stockholm, Sweden on October 9, 1970. Her name is pronounced "Ah-nick-ah Soreen-stahm." She started playing golf at the age of twelve. While playing as an amateur she was a member of the Swedish National Golf Team from 1987 to 1992 and was the World Amateur Champion in 1992.

Annika is 5-feet 6-inches tall, has blonde hair and typical Nordic blue eyes. She is a slim 125 pounds, a delicate looking young lady. One would never suspect that she has Ben Hogan-like skills at golf. She is cool, restrained, a bit shy, unemotional and never shows temper. She has her emotions under complete control at all times.

Annika was married on January 4, 1997 to David Esch, a representative of a golf equipment manufacturer.

Annika attended the University of Arizona and won seven collegiate titles while she was in school. She was the 1991 College Player of the Year as well as the N.C.A.A. champion. In 1992 she was named to the N.C.A.A. All-American golf team.

She joined the LPGA in 1993. Annika was not an overnight success as a pro. In 1994 she competed in eighteen LPGA tournaments, but she did not chalk up a single victory. Her best showing was a tie for second.

However, she was named "Rookie of the Year" on the strength of her three top-10 finishes. She started to move up the money ladder, too, with a total of $127,457 in earnings.

Her game peaked 1995-1997. In fact, she dominated the LPGA Tour in much the fashion that Nancy Lopez did when she burst onto the Tour in 1978 with nine victories.

Annika became the number 1 money-winner on the L.P.G.A. Tour in 1995 with $666,533. In 1995 she was awarded the "Athlete of the Year" award in Sweden, Sweden's most prestigious award in sports.

She was again leading money-winner in 1996 with $808,311 and repeated again in 1997 with her first million-dollar year, $1,236,789.

In 1997 Annika crossed the two million milestone in career earnings after her victory in the Longs Drug Challenge. She was the fastest player in LPGA history to accomplish that feat. It took her just three years, one month and eighteen days to reach that tremendous sum.

Since Annika won her first title on the LPGA Tour at the 1995 U.S. Women's Open she has missed only two cuts in forty-eight starts, a marvelous achievement.

Annika has picked up a little extra change, too, by winning the J.C. Penney Skins Tournament in 1997. Her total winnings there were $220,000 as she outdueled Laura Davies, Karrie Webb and Dottie Pepper.

Annika has one of the sweetest swings in women's golf. She swings in such leisurely fashion that one would expect a nice ladylike 185 to 190-yard drive at most. But there is explosive power at the bottom of the swing that propels the drive to an average of 237 yards, moderately long and most importantly very straight. She uses the biggest Calloway "Big Bertha" and the Maxfli "Revolution" ball.

She is able to reach many of the shorter 5-pars in two strokes for birdies or eagles. She is a deadly putter especially from ten feet or less from the hole.

Here are some of the highlights of Annika Sorenstam's career:

1994 Rolex Rookie of the Year

1995 First foreign player to win the Vare trophy for the lowest scoring average of 71.00 strokes per round.

1995 With $666,533 in season's earnings she was the leading money-winner.

1995 When she won the 1995 U.S. Women's Open she became the Thirteenth LPGA player to win the Open as her first LPGA victory.

1995 Won the Samsung World Championship of Women's Golf in an extra-hole match defeating Laura Davies, for her third career victory.

1995 Won the CHP Heartland Classic by ten strokes, the largest margin of victory on the LPGA Tour that year.

1996 Won her second Vare Trophy for lowest season scoring average with 70.47.

1996 Won her second World Championship of Women's Golf.

1996 Successfully defended her title at the U.S. Women's scoring four rounds of par or better, 70-67-69-66 and surpassed $1,000,000 in earnings.

Prediction: Annika Sorenstam will dominate the LPGA Tour for years to come.

DAVID DUVAL

David Robert Duval was born on November 9, 1971 in Jacksonville, Florida. He is 6-feet tall and weighs 190 pounds. He is not married.

David has three PGA Tour victories, the Michelob Championship at Kingsmill, Virginia, the Walt Disney World Oldsmobile Classic and the Tour Championship, all won in 1997. In 1997 he finished in second place on the PGA Tour standings with earnings of $1,885,308, an incredible sum in view of the fact that three years previously in 1994 he had won only $44,006.00 and had finished 195th in the standings.

What was the reason for the meteoric rise of David Duval? The answer is self-discipline. Five years ago David weighed 235 pounds. He realized that while he had an excellent golf swing his weight was interfering with his ability to "close" a tournament. Frequently he would tire in the last few holes and would have a few crucial bad shots.

Amazingly, he played in eighty-six PGA Tour events before he finally broke through and won his first, the Mercedes Championship.

Let's go back to his early career and see how he developed into the star golfer he now is. David played his college golf at Georgia Tech, a well-known birthplace of future great golfers such as Davis Love III, Larry Mize and Stuart Cink. While he was at Georgia Tech he was named four times in a row to the first team All-America. Only Gary Hallberg and Phil Mickelson had matched that fine record before David. David was named Collegiate "Player of the Year" in 1993, a designation which foretold a bright career for him when he turned pro that year.

In 1993 David played in five PGA events and barely made a living. He earned only $27,181 that year and was an also-ran at 201st place in the Tour standings. David struggled for two years before he "found his game" in 1995. He made thirty-six out of forty-nine cuts in 1995 and vaulted into the top ten money-winners in 1997 with a total of $1,850,000. Until late in 1997 he had not yet won a tournament. The press was on his back calling him an "also-ran" who could not finish with a victory when he had the chance to do so.

At that point in his life David decided he would have to change his physical appearance. He took several months off and worked strenuously with weights, exercise and a strict low calorie diet. The result was a slimmed down David Duval.

Sometimes a new slim body does not work quite as well as the old stout one did. The golfer has to adapt to his new flatter stomach and thus make adjustments in the swing that has been working well for years. David lost thirty pounds. He did not succeed at once with his new slimmer body. It took months of practice until he felt secure with his "new" swing. His confidence rose and his scores showed improvement.

Everyone in the sports field kept asking him "David, when are you going to win a tournament?" David finally answered his critics in fine fashion at the 1997 Mercedes Championship at Kingsmill, Williamsburg, Virginia.

Duffy Waldorf started off the first day of the tournament with an 8-under par-63 to lead Brad Bryant by a stroke. David had a 67 on his first round and followed with a 66-133.

Waldorf came back with a 69 for 132 and led David by one stroke. Bryant fell off with a bad 76 and eventually tied for fifteenth place.

Waldorf produced an excellent 69, his second in a row. Waldorf was then at 12-under par, three strokes ahead of David and three other players in pursuit of Waldorf, Grant Waite, a New Zealander, Fred Funk and Kirt Triplett.

The weather turned cooler and windier for the final round. Playing in front of Waldorf, David shot a strong 67 that last day and then stood by to watch Waldorf return a steady 70 to tie him at 271.

At last David had a chance to win his first tournament and he did so with a ten-foot birdie putt on the first extra hole. He had broken the second-place jinx at last. His purse was $279,000. He had finished second seven times before he finally captured his first victory.

With new-found confidence, David proceeded to win his next two events as well, an unheard-of feat in modern day professional golf.

Let's look at David Duval, the man. He gives the impression that he is cool, distant, unsmiling. He has an air of confidence, even cockiness. Perhaps it is simply confidence as a result of knowing that he has at last arrived and can match his game with the best of the other golfers.

He has an odd shape for a golfer, a long body and short stubby, heavy legs. It is his legs, no doubt, that give him the tremendous power he has with his driver. David averages 280.1 yards per drive, only a few yards in distance behind Eldrick "Tiger" Woods who averaged 294.9 during the 1997 season.

David wears contact lenses. The glare of sunlight bothers his eyes so he wears dark, wrap-around sunglasses to help with the problem.

David is reported to be a loner. He does not fraternize with the other professionals and is often observed eating alone or with his caddie as his companion.

Another indication of his unusual personality is that he affects a scrawny mustache and goatee for a number of months and then suddenly will appear smooth-shaven for a while. Then he will let the goatee and beard grow again. Perhaps David Duval has not decided what image he wishes to project to the world.

Curtis Strange, two-time U.S. Open champion and now a respected television golf commentator, recently said: "The fiercest rivalry over the next ten years will be Tiger Woods versus David Duval. I believe that Duval will be the one player who will consistently be Woods's strongest adversary in big tournament situations. David has the discipline and the will to be one of the best players in the world."

PHIL MICKELSON

Philip Alfred Mickelson was born on June 16, 1970 in San Diego, California. He is 6-feet 2-inches tall and weighs 190 pounds.

Phil's father claims that the young Phil hit his first golf balls at the age of eighteen months. He is right-handed in everything but golf. He became a left-handed golfer when his father, who himself was a good golfer, demonstrated the swing right-handed and Phil mimicked his swing left-handed.

Phil first came to national attention when he won the 1990 U.S. Amateur. He had already won the N.C.A.A. Championship while a student at Arizona State. Only Phil, Jack Nicklaus and Tiger Woods have won the N.C.A.A. and the U.S. Amateur in the same year. Along with Gary Hallberg and David Duval, Phil was a fourth-time first team college golf All-American.

As a leading amateur, Phil was invited to nineteen PGA Tour tournaments. He made nine cuts. He was gaining great experience and becoming accustomed to matching his game against the pros.

The outstanding accomplishment of his amateur golf career came in 1991 when he won the Nortel Open. It was practically unheard of that an amateur would win a professional tournament. After he had turned pro, he won the Telecom Open again in 1995, a rare feat, winning the same tournament twice, first as an amateur and then as a pro.

Phil turned pro in June, 1992 and went on to prosper on the PGA Tour. He has now won eleven titles in the United States and one overseas, the 1993 Perrier Open in France. He was the fourth youngest professional at twenty-six years, nine months to win ten titles on the PGA Tour.

In 1995 he shot an opening score of 65 at the Masters, the
lowest score by a left-hander in Masters history, and he eventually finished third.

After he joined the PGA Tour in June 1992, he played in ten
events that year. He did not win one. His earnings were only
$171,714 as he finished nintieth in rank on the tour.

1993 was a better year as he won twice, the Buick
Invitational at Torrey Pines, San Diego, California and the
prestigious International Tournament in which the most
prominent players from all around the world participate. Phil's
earnings that year reached $628,735.

Phil continued to improve his standing on the Tour, and in
1996 he broke the million dollar mark, broke it soundly, too,
with $1,697,799 in earnings.

That year he won the Nortel Open, the Phoenix Open, the
GTE Byron Nelson Classic and the NEC World Series of Golf.
By winning the World Series with its first prize of $378,000,
the largest he had ever won, he earned an exempt status on
the Tour through the year 2006.

Let's look at the golf swing and putting style of Phil
Mickelson. The first thing an observer notices is that Phil, with
apparently little effort, drives the ball prodigious distances. He
averages 284 yards per drive according to PGA statistics, just
ten yards less than his famous competitor, Eldrick "Tiger"
Woods. That driving distance means that nearly all 5-par
holes are well within the reach of Mickelson in two strokes for
possible eagles, probable birdies.

His touch around the green is nothing less than miraculous.
He has mastered what is known as the "flop shot" with his
sand wedge.

The sand wedge is usually a 60º club in most golf bags. Phil
uses one with 63º loft. The result of a mighty swing through
deep rough 50 to 60 yards from the green is a ball that shoots
straight up into the air. From the force of the swing the
onlooker is certain that the ball will fly many yards farther
than the intended flagstick but, no, it settles down softly and
invariably near the hole.

Phil has been able to perform this shot so many times under pressure that the galleries are accustomed to seeing him do it. It is a most exciting shot to watch and Phil is the master of the technique.

When Phil won the Nortel Open as an amateur he showed his ability to overcome adversity, to persevere and ultimately win.

As he played the fourteenth hole on his last round he had a one stroke lead over Tom Purtzer, a 39 year old veteran in his seventeenth season on the Tour, and Bob Tway who is eleven years older than Phil and winner of the 1986 PGA Championship.

After visiting the desert and a bunker, Phil left the green with a dreaded "snowman," an 8, and was three strokes behind Purtzer and Tway.

But Purtzer, playing ahead of Phil, lost the lead when he hit his second shot into a bunker, failed to extricate the ball on his first try and took a double-bogey-6. Tway, playing the seventeenth, missed the green to the left and failed to sink a 10-foot par-saving putt.

At the sixteenth, Mickelson knew what he had to do to win, birdie two of the last three holes. He performed his magical "flop shot" at the sixteenth hole and put his ball one foot from the hole for the first birdie he needed. Then at the par-4 eighteenth he hit a sparkling second shot to within eight feet of the hole. Of course, he made the putt to win and be the first amateur winner of a PGA event since Scott Verplank did it in 1985 at the Western Open.

Phil Mickelson is one of the "sweetest" golfers to appear on the PGA Tour in years. He has a constant, appealing smile and never shows temper when a shot or putt goes astray.

He is tall, strong and his swing is a beautiful one—long and leisurely on the backswing and then amazingly powerful through the ball to a high full follow-through. Furthermore, he repeats this swing time after time after time.

Ben Crenshaw, a fellow professional, is acknowledged to be one of the finest putters of all time. Phil Mickelson studied Crenshaw's method carefully and has accomplished a remarkable duplication of Crenshaw's putting style. He even uses the left-handed counterpart of Crenshaw's Wilson Model 8802 putter. Incidentally, Arnold Palmer used the right-handed model of the 8802 for many of his early triumphs.

According to Crenshaw, "There is nobody who has better natural skills and a feeling for the game than Phil Mickelson. His imagination and ability to create shots rivals that of Severiano Ballesteros, a recognized master of the short game. Besides that his competitive desire is among the strongest I've ever seen."

Phil is a licensed pilot of propeller-driven planes and recently qualified to fly jet planes. It is likely that we will soon see Phil fly his own private jet plane to the tournaments and park it alongside those of Jack Nicklaus and Greg Norman.

Phil and his wife, Amy, a beautiful, fragile woman, tiny alongside Phil's 6-foot 2-inch height, have a brand-new house in Paradise Valley, Arizona. The house is designed for a sports lover like Phil. They have a swimming pool, of course, and a most unusual water slide which Phil had constructed from a small mountain that rises above and behind the house in back. There is a regulation putting green, too, you may be sure, to hone Phil's silky stroke. He keeps it at twelve on the Stimpmeter, the device that measures the speed of a putting green. Twelve is very fast, about U.S. Open and Masters speed.

All in all, life is very pleasant for the Mickelsons in their Paradise Valley. Prediction: Phil Mickelson will win his first major tournament in the near future and will continue to be one of the brightest stars of the PGA Tour.

ERNIE ELS

Theodore Ernest Els was born October 17, 1969 in Johannesburg, South Africa. he is 6-feet 3-inches tall and weighs 210 pounds. In his early years Ernie Els (his last name is pronounced "else") was a good tennis player with a hundred- mile-an-hour serve.

Although he played tennis until he was fourteen, he had discovered the game of golf when he was only nine years old. When he was fourteen he made his mind up. Golf was more interesting and challenging, so he quit tennis completely and began to develop what has turned out to be one of the smoothest, most effective swings in golf history.

Els, a big man, is easy-going, laid-back, slow-moving, and never seems to get ruffled or excited no matter how badly or how well his game is going. He has the air of a great big happy St. Bernard, just delighted that he is succeeding at his favorite game.

His swing is simple, smooth and appears to be effortless. Still, he is one of the longest drivers of modern golf with an average of 270 yards per try.

He became a professional golfer in 1989 at the age of twenty. He came to the United States in 1990. He had some lean years at first. In 1991 his total earnings were only $8,790 from one tournament on the NIKE Tour and one on the PGA Tour.

Contrast that with his tremendous winnings of $1,243,008, which he earned in 1997. Ernie now has five PGA Tour victories and has already won two major titles, the 1994 and 1997 U.S. Open championships. He is the first foreign player to accomplish this golf "double" since Alex Smith, a Scot, who won the titles twice in 1906 and 1910.

The 1994 U.S. Open was played at Oakmont Country Club in Oakmont, Pennsylvania. Els, with 279, tied Colin Montgomerie, the Scot, and Loren Roberts for the lead at the end of 72 holes.

In a dramatic eighteenth hole playoff Els scored a 74 to tie Roberts who also had a 74. Montgomerie fell by the wayside with a 78 and was eliminated. The play continued in sudden death overtime. Els prevailed as he scored 4-4 to Roberts' 4-5 to Roberts' 4-5. Els had won his first major title.

In the 1997 U.S. Open at the Blue Course of Congressional Country Club in Bethesda, Maryland, four players had the tournament in reach as they made the turn on the final round, all tied at 4-under par. They were Els, Colin Montgomerie, Jeff Maggert and Tom Lehman.

Els was the only one who matched par the rest of the way. Maggert fell off quickly with a three-putt at the thirteenth, a bogey at sixteen and a double bogey at seventeen. Montgomerie was tied with Els at the seventeenth, a 480-yard downhill 4-par with a pond on the left side of the green, the flagstick dangerously near the water. He played the hole too cautiously, missed the green, chipped and left himself a five-foot putt for par.

Colin waited nearly five minutes before he putted, distracted by the crowd noise and movement around the eighteenth green which was visible nearby. Montgomerie's putt never came close to holing and he was out of it.

Lehman was a stroke behind Els as he played the seventeenth hole. He attacked the pin at seventeen, got a little greedy trying to get the ball close to the hole and, to his dismay, saw the ball splash into the pond. He, too was out of the chase.

In the final round, Els holed a chip shot at ten to tie for the lead. Then he seized it outright with a birdie at the twelfth but gave it back with a bogey at thirteen. Then he played steadily in hitting fairways and greens and sank a testing four-footer for his par at the last hole and his second U.S. Open title.

Els said later that he thought his strength out of the heavy rough was the key to his success in both Opens.

For Els, it was the sweetest victory of his life. His smooth- as-butter swing, his steady, accurate putting stroke and his incredible patience in the face of adversity never left him.

"When I won the Open in 1994, I said if people would be patient with me, I'd win another one and I have."

There is no doubt that Ernie Els should now be considered one of the modern day superstars of golf.

GREG NORMAN

G regory John Norman was born on February 10, 1955 in Queensland, Australia. his father, Mervyn, and mother Toini, were both of Nordic ancestry.

Greg's father was an electrical engineer. He had a strong personality and was disappointed when he could not motivate Greg to work hard at his studies. Greg, for the most part, was an avid surfer who spent hours on end in the waves.

On a skin-diving trip when he was in his teens Greg fell into the hold of the boat and broke off two of his front teeth. He nearly became a "station hand," an Aussie cowboy, before he discovered the attraction of the game of golf.

Greg got his first set of golf clubs when he was fifteen and by the time he was seventeen he was a scratch golfer, that is, a par-shooter. From the start he could drive the ball tremendous distances and was on nearly all the 5-par holes in two shots.

He happened to read Jack Nicklaus's book *Golf My Way*. He studied it and adopted much of Jack's instruction in the golf swing into his own game.

After he was nearly drowned in a surfing accident, he turned his attention completely to golf. He even told his friends at that time, "Before I'm thirty I'm going to be a millionaire at golf." It turned out that he was speaking the truth.

Greg practiced golf five hours a day. He became an assistant pro at the Beverly Park Golf Club in Sydney where he was allowed to polish his game on the practice tee.

He became an overnight success when he won his first professional tournament, the West Lakes Classic which had a $35,000 purse. His prize was $7,000 on rounds of 64, 67, 67 and 74. He was twelve shots ahead of the field at the end of

164 the third round. Greg said afterwards: "I thought I was the richest man in the world."

In 1974 Greg went to America to try his skills on the American PGA tour. On an American Airline flight from Detroit to New York he was served by a pretty stewardess named Laura Andrassy. With both of them it was truly a case of love at first sight.

Greg recalls: "I remember telling James Marshall, my agent, who was traveling with me: "I'll bet you I marry that woman. And I never even met her."

In 1981, Greg married Laura at St. Mary's Catholic Church in Old Town, Alexandria, Virginia. They now have two children, a daughter Morgan Leigh, born on October 5, 1982 and a son, Gregory, born September 19, 1985.

Greg was not an instant success in America. It took him five years to win his first tournament, the 1984 Kemper Open. The prize was $72,000, ten times the amount of his first victory in Australia.

Greg got his nickname, "The Shark" when an Augusta, Georgia newspaperman heard him say, in an interview, that his recreation was chasing and shooting great white sharks off the barrier reef of Australia.

The Augusta Chronicle headline the next day read: "Great White Shark leads Masters."

Everyone remembers the remarkable victory of Jack Nicklaus in the 1986 Masters, the heart-warming sight of Jack hugging his son, Jackie, his caddie on the eighteenth green after the last putt had been holed. Jack was in with a score of 279 on a final round of 65.

But what most people have forgotten is that Greg Norman made a tremendous run at Jack in that same tournament.

After Greg suffered a double-bogey at the tenth hole on his final round, he fought back valiantly. He birdied the 5-par thirteenth when he was on in two and took two putts. He had only a 140-yard second shot to the 5-par fifteenth. He counted a birdie there and then nearly holed his tee shot to the sixteenth with a curling tee shot only three feet from the hole. He made the deuce, of course.

Greg had a bad tee shot to the left at the seventeenth, but he improvised a magical run-up shot from under a tree in the rough to twelve feet from the hole. Norman sank that putt and was then tied with Nicklaus who was already in with his 65 and 279 total.

All Greg had to do was par the eighteenth hole to tie Jack Nicklaus. However, after a good tee shot on eighteen Greg made a poor swing on his second shot and saw his ball tail to the right into the crowd around the eighteenth green.

His chip to the hole was a very difficult one from a downhill lie to a green which sloped away from him. He did the best he could but his ball went fifteen feet past the hole. Greg did not make that putt so his chance to tie for the Masters title was gone. He finished second in a tie with Tom Kite who also had a final putt to tie Nicklaus for the lead but, sadly, saw his putt slip by the hole.

In 1987 Greg thought he had the Masters title won. Seve Ballesteros and Larry Mize, had already finished, tied at 285.

Mize was a young journeyman golfer who had risen to the height of his ability and had finished his round with a six-footer for a birdie at the eighteenth, tying Ballesteros who had already finished.

Greg needed a twenty-two-foot putt to win outright but he failed to hole it.

The three players, Mize, Ballesteros and Norman proceeded to the tenth tee for a "sudden death" playoff. Seve bogied the hole when he three-putted the tenth green. Greg and Larry made pars and went to the eleventh hole, leaving Ballesteros in tears to climb up the long hill to the clubhouse.

At the eleventh, after a good second shot to the green, Greg left himself a 50-foot putt but he was confident he could two-putt for par and probably win. For Mize, on the other hand, had hit a second shot to the right of the green and was 140 feet away from the flagstick with a downhill pitch to the green which sloped severely away from him.

Mize had an "impossible" shot but he made the best stroke he ever made in his life. He clipped a sand wedge into the fringe of the green. The ball took two bounces in the longer grass which slowed its progress nicely. The ball ran straight for the hole and bang against the flagstick for a most improbable birdie-3.

Mize jumped into the air with delight when he saw the ball go in. Norman did not sink his putt for a tying 3 and Mize was the winner of the 1987 Masters, Norman once more a runner-up.

Greg Norman has now won eighteen PGA Tour victories and has won a phenomenal fifty-five times in the international field. His titles include the British Open twice, at Turnberry in 1986 and at Royal St. George's when he closed with a 74 to defeat Nick Faldo by two strokes.

In 1996 at the Masters tournament Nick Faldo got a measure of revenge when he came from six strokes behind Norman and shot a final round of 67 as Greg "lost his game" and stumbled to a 78.

Greg Norman has had five million-dollar years in a row and has amassed nearly twelve million dollars in tournament earnings through 1997.

Greg Norman has come a long way from the days of his surfing in Australia. He is undoubtedly one of the finest golfers who has ever played the game.

"TIGER" WOODS

"**P**henom," n., a person of phenomenal ability or promise. Truly Eldrick "Tiger" Woods is a phenom (pronounced, fee-nom) of the present golf world.

In the 1920s and 1930s it was the field against Robert T. "Bobby" Jones. In the 1950s it was Ben Hogan against the field. Then Arnold Palmer and Jack Nicklaus became the overwhelming favorites in the 70s and 80s.

It is estimated that an extra 10,000 people will attend a golf tournament just to witness Tiger's 125 mile-an-hour swing propel the ball three hundred yards or more. What's more, he drives the ball straight. And has the touch of a brain surgeon in and around the greens.

Eldrick "Tiger" Woods was born on December 30, 1975, the son and first-born child of Earl and Kutilda Woods. His mother, called "Tida," devised his name from a combination of the first letters of his parents' first names.

Lieutenant Colonel Earl Woods was on his second tour of duty in Vietnam. Twice his life had been saved by an early warning of danger from Nguyen T. Phong, his counterpart in the Vietnamese army.

Tiger's father, Earl, had said, "He (Phong) was special in combat so I began calling him "Tiger." But after Earl returned from Viet Nam he never heard from Phong again.

Woods never forgot his debt to Phong and vowed that if he were ever blessed with another child, a son he hoped, he would call him "Tiger" as a tribute to Phong and to keep his memory alive.

Woods was nearly fifty years old and a divorced man with three children from an earlier marriage when he met a young pretty Thai woman, Kutilda Punsawad, in Bangkok. He brought her back to the United States and shortly thereafter married her in 1965. Woods had been exposed to the game of golf when he was stationed at Fort Hamilton, in Brooklyn, New York. He fell in love with the game and made up his mind that if he ever had another child he or she would play the game of golf earlier than he did.

Along came Tiger. Earl started his new son in golf at a precocious age. At the age of two, Tiger was entered into a competition for boys 10 and under. And he won. When he was three he broke 50 for the first time.

When Tiger was four years old, the golf pro at Hartwell Golf Park in Long Beach, California took one look at his swing and said, "I was blown away. It was unbelievable. He had a perfect address position and took his club back into a perfect position at the top every time."

When Tiger was five he had a full set of clubs which were cut down, of course, to his size. The television show *That's Incredible* featured him in one of the broadcasts hitting Whiffle balls into the audience.

At the age of eight, he won the Junior World ten-and-under division. He won it again at nine, the eleven and twelve division at twelve. In 1987 he was undefeated, having won thirty Junior tournaments.

Fast forward to the 1994 U.S. Amateur, Tiger's first major championship. In the final round Tiger's opponent was Trip Kuehne, a senior at Oklahoma State. They knew each other well, having played in many Junior tournaments together.

Kuehne birdied seven of the first thirteen holes to open what appeared to be an insurmountable lead. By lunch time the deficit was four holes.

Playing the second eighteen, Kuehne was still five up with twelve to play. By the tenth hole Woods had struck back and was only one down. At the sixteenth, Tiger holed a five-foot putt for a birdie to even the match. The seventeenth hole at the TPC at Sawgrass, Ponte Vedra, Florida is a famous island green, completely surrounded by water.

Tiger hit a smooth, soft fade with his pitching wedge to the green 139 yards away. He saw his ball settle down on the green only eighteen inches from watery disaster, but fourteen feet away from a birdie-2. While the whole world of golf watched on TV, he sank that putt and was one up with one hole to play. The eighteenth hole was anti-climactic when Kuehne missed a 6-foot par putt. Tiger was the new U.S. Amateur champion, the youngest of all time.

The next important event in Tiger's career occurred at the 1995 U.S. Amateur at Newport Country Club. Only eight players had ever won the title in successive years, Bobby Jones among them.

This time Tiger practically murdered the field. Only one opponent reached the eighteenth green. In the final round Tiger ran into stiff opposition in George Marucci, Jr., a forty-three-year-old investment consultant and Mercedes dealer. Through twelve holes in the 36-hole match, Tiger was three down but only one down at lunch time.

By the thirteenth hole Tiger was two up with three to play. Tiger closed the match with a second shot to the last green only eighteen inches from the hole. He had won the U.S. Amateur championship for the second time.

Tiger went on to win his third U.S. Amateur championship, defeating Steve Scott from the University of Florida at the Ghost Creek course at Pumpkin Ridge, Oregon.

In the final round Scott was up five up on Woods at the end of the first eighteen holes. Scott continued to lead by two with three holes to play. It appeared that Tiger's winning streak was about to end.

Then Tiger calmly holed a crucial 30-foot putt on the seventeenth hole when he had to make it to stay alive in the match. Tiger won on the second extra hole with a sparkling tee shot only seven feet from the 3-par hole.

Jack Nicklaus and Arnold Palmer played a practice round with Tiger in preparation for the 1996 Masters. Tiger was eligible for the tournament because he was a past U.S. Amateur champion. Robert T. "Bobby" Jones, Jr. always invited lead-

ing amateurs to his tournament because he felt that in that
way he was helping to promote amateur golf as a whole.

After the round, Jack told the press "Both Arnold and I agree that you could take my six Masters and his four Masters victories, add them all together and this kid should win more than that." Nicklaus, of course, could not anticipate what Tiger would do to the Augusta National course when he won the 1997 Masters.

It was time for Tiger to make the decision to declare himself a professional golfer, as they say, "Turn Pro."

Within days of his announcement he had signed endorsement contracts with NIKE, American Express and Titleist, the golf ball and club manufacturer, worth an estimated $40,000,000 over the next few years.

In a *Wall Street Journal* ad Tiger told the world: "I shot in the 70s when I was eight. I won the Junior Amateur when I was fourteen. I won the U.S. Amateur when I was eighteen. I am the only man to win three consecutive U.S. Amateur titles. Are you ready for me?"

Tiger quickly established himself on the PGA Tour with the finest start a rookie had ever made. He won twice in 1996 and four times in 1997 and earned an astounding $2,066,833 in 1997 alone.

The highlight of his performance came at the 1997 Masters tournament. He had played in the 1995 and 1996 tournaments but had not done well. He tied for forty-first in 1995 and missed the cut in 1996.

This time, Tiger came in more experienced and determined to win. Off to a shaky start with four bogeys on the first nine, he recovered and scored a 6-under par-30 on the second nine, a first round of 70. Then he proceeded to demolish the course with scores of 66, 65 and 69, 18 strokes under par, 270, a score which broke the tournament record of 171 set by Jack Nicklaus and Raymond Floyd.

Here is the hole-by-hole score of Tiger Woods as he won the 1997 Masters, one of the finest performances in the history of golf:

TIGER WOODS ROUND-BY-ROUND

Hole	1	2	3	4	5	6	7	8	9	Out	10	11	12	13	14	15	16	17	18	In	Total
Par	4	5	4	3	4	3	4	5	4	36	4	4	3	5	4	5	3	4	4	36	72
Round 1	5	5	4	4	4	3	4	6	5	40	3	4	2	4	4	3	3	3	4	30	70
Status	+1	+1	+1	+2	+2	+2	+2	+3	+4		+3	+3	+2	+1	+1	−1	−1	−2	−2		
Round 2	4	4	5	3	3	3	4	4	4	34	4	4	3	3	3	4	3	4	4	32	66
Status	−2	−3	−2	−2	−3	−3	−3	−4	−4		−4	−4	−4	−6	−7	−8	−8	−8	−8		
Round 3	4	4	4	3	3	3	3	4	4	32	4	3	3	5	4	4	3	4	3	33	65
Status	−8	−9	−9	−9	−10	−10	−11	−12	−12		−12	−13	−13	−13	−13	−14	−14	−14	−15		
Round 4	4	4	4	3	5	3	5	4	4	36	4	3	3	4	3	5	3	4	4	33	69
Status	−15	−16	−16	−16	−15	−15	−14	−15	−15		−15	−16	−16	−17	−18	−18	−18	−18	−18		270

With drives that averaged 323 yards and hitting pitching
wedges into 5-par holes, Tiger was in complete control of his
game. He had won his first major championship in smashing
fashion. The whole world saw him in tears as he embraced his
father, Earl, at greenside of the eighteenth hole of Augusta
National Golf course.

Where will Tiger go from here? Will he win the eleven
Masters titles Jack Nicklaus predicted for him? Only time
will tell.

NANCY LOPEZ

Nancy Marie Lopez was born in Torrance, California on January 6, 1951. Her parents were Marina and Domingo Lopez, Mexican-Americans. Domingo, nicknamed "Sunday" (the translation of his name in Spanish) was a low handicap golfer and was Nancy's only golf coach.

Nancy's mother also played golf and encouraged the young Nancy to play when she was a small child.

Nancy had an older sister, Delma, who was twelve when Nancy was born. Delma married early so, in effect, Nancy was an only child.

Nancy is 5-feet 4^1/$_2$-inches tall and weighs about 145 pounds. She is truly the "Madonna" of modern women's golf, an animated pretty brunette with a gorgeous clear complexion and sparkling eyes.

She is married to Ray Knight, the former baseball player who recently was the manager of the Cincinnati Reds baseball team. The Knights have three beautiful daughters.

Nancy's mother died suddenly and unexpectedly after an appendix operation that went wrong. Nancy was only eighteen years old at the time and her death was a great shock to her and to her father.

Nancy inherited her mother's golf clubs at an early age. From the start Nancy was a golfing prodigy. She played and practiced at a public golf course in Roswell, New Mexico.

At the age of twelve, Nancy won the New Mexico Women's Amateur Championship playing against grown-up women golfers of considerable skill.

In 1972, only fifteen years old, she won the USGA Girls Junior Championship. On her way to the finals she required only 55 holes to win four matches, an average of 14 holes per match. Nancy won the same title again in 1974, defeating Lauren Howe 7 and 6 in the final round at Columbia Edgewater Country Club in Portland, Oregon.

Nancy's excellent amateur golf record earned her a scholarship to Arizona State College. She drove a 177 Gran Torino when she was in college. She was called "Skeetch Lopez" because she liked to spin the wheels of her car when she took off.

Nancy was also a C.B. radio addict. Her handle was "Jive Cookie" connoting the fact that she was hung up on disco, jazz and rock music.

Nancy was in college less than a year when she decided to try her luck on the Ladies Professional Tour. Just twenty years old, she became an instant success.

She entered twelve events and won five tournaments in a row. She was either first or second in nine of those twelve. She earned nearly half a million dollars ($470,386) that first year.

Nancy recently reminisced about her sensational first year in 1978. Since she had a fine amateur career it might have been expected that she would win a tournament or two. But nine victories, including the LPGA championship?

"It seems incredible now, Nancy says, "I was definitely in a zone. Every shot went where I wanted to hit it. Every putt went where I wanted to putt it."

"Everything got easier and easier. I was swinging so well. I wasn't afraid of anybody or anything."

"I wasn't afraid to putt it by the hole. If I missed I made it coming back."

Nancy became a superstar practically overnight. She rode in limousines and private planes and was in demand for television interviews.

At the end of the year Nancy had won both Rookie of the Year and Player of the Year honors, the Vare Trophy for lowest scoring average and nearly $190,000 in prize money.

When Nancy won the 1985 LPGA championship at the Jack Nicklaus Golf Club at King's Island, Ohio, she had a

remarkable string of holes, one that may never again be
equaled. She shot an eagle, birdie, par, par, birdie, eagle, par, birdie, birdie, 8-under par for ten holes, a round of 65.

Let's take a look at Nancy's swing. Nancy herself says: "I have a very slow tempo which I feel reduces the margin of error. I try very hard to take the club back low and slow.

The fact is that Nancy has a distinctly individual swing. She has an unusual hitch in her swing, peculiarly her own. When she addresses the ball she holds her hands low and then as she begins her backswing she lifts them straight upward. She keeps her left heel firmly on the ground during the backswing, an action which firms up her left side and allows her to wind up the big muscles of the body against her left leg. She has a beautiful full follow-through, a sweeping extension of her swing.

Nancy was aware of the fact that she had a "different swing," so she sought out Lee Trevino one time for advice on whether she should change it.

Lee told her, "You can't argue with success. If you swing badly but still score and win, don't change a thing." Nancy stayed with her own style and prospered.

When Nancy won her thirty-fifth victory in 1987 she qualified for the LPGA Hall of Fame. She was inducted in July, 1987 as the eleventh member of that distinguished group.

In 1988 she was the second player to cross the $2,000,000 mark in career earnings, the fourth player ever to top that barrier.

In a twenty year long career Nancy has won 48 times on the LPGA tour and has earned more than $5,000,000 through 1997. She was named "Golfer of the Decade" by *Golf* magazine for the years 1978–1987 during the Centennial of Golf celebration in 1988. She also won the 1998 Bob Jones Award which recognizes distinguished sportsmanship in golf.

Nancy Lopez is, without question, one of the finest women golfers of all time.

JUSTIN LEONARD

With the era of the modern "Big Three" of golf, Arnold Palmer, Jack Nicklaus, and Gary Player, coming to an end, golf experts predicted that a new breed of superstars would appear and dominate the golf world. These new stars would be supermen, big and strong and would drive the golf ball stupendous distances.

That prediction seems to have come true for we have seen four new stars who fit the "super-golfer" specifications.

These superstars of today and probably tomorrow are Phil Mickelson, 6-feet 2-inches tall; Ernie Els, 6-feet 3-inches tall, Eldrick "Tiger" Woods, 6-feet 2-inches tall; and David Duval, an even 6-feet tall.

It is somewhat of a surprise to find a true David among these four Goliaths. Justin Charles Garret Leonard is the new David who is not only challenging the Goliaths of present day golf but knocking them down with regularity.

Justin was born June 15, 1972 in Dallas, Texas. He is 5-feet 9-inches tall and weighs 160 pounds. However, he has a body of tooled steel that he has turned into an efficient golfing machine.

Justin grew up in Texas, and from his early days was influenced by the mystique of Ben Hogan who lived nearby. He decided to take Hogan as his model, and a wise decision it has turned out to be.

Justin adopted the Hogan method of practice. That is, the early morning sun found him on the practice range and the setting sun was his signal to quit for the day.

Justin felt that Ben Hogan was the best club designer so he played, and plays, Ben Hogan clubs. He even adopted the Ben Hogan flat white visor cap to help him complete the Hogan image and remind him of his idol.

179

Justin is a quiet man, some say even an introvert. He smiles rarely and shows an intensity of concentration in his play that few other players have.

Justin's dedication to making his golf game a success has paid off wonderfully, as we shall see.

The wellknown teacher of golf, Randy Smith, commented on Justin Leonard's swing recently. He said, "The cornerstone of Justin Leonard's swing is the exceptional balance he exhibits from start to finish. His powerful right-side release carries his body into a low and left finish position."

Justin has a highly individual style of putting. But it is an effective one, as evidenced by his putting under pressure at the 1997 British Open where he holed several 20 to 25 foot putts when he had to do so to win.

Justin makes his first appraisal of the putting line and distance from behind the ball. Then he steps into his stance and places his putter on line. His eyes are not directly over the ball as many good teachers advise but are well inside the line.

Then comes the odd action. He steps away from the ball completely and again reviews the situation from behind the ball. Once again he reassembles his stance and at last strokes the ball. Who can argue with a method that apparently works for Justin Leonard?

Justin first came to national attention when he won the 1992 U.S. Amateur Championship. He was only a twenty year-old Junior at the University of Texas when he encountered Thomas Scherrer in the 36 hole final of the event.

Leonard simply demolished Scherrer and won by a score of 8 and 7, one of the most one-sided victories in the history of the tournament.

In 1994, at the age of twenty-two, after his U.S. Amateur victory, Justin decided to turn pro. He received a number of invitations from sponsors to play in the PGA Tour. By winning enough prize money he was able to earn his PGA Tour card without ever having to go through the torture of the PGA qualifying school.

Having turned pro in 1994, Justin took two years to estab-

lish himself as a player to watch. In 1995 he finished second
twice and earned three-quarters of a million dollars.

Then he broke through with a vengeance in 1996 when he made twenty-three cuts of twenty-nine and came near the million dollar mark with $943,140,000 in earnings.

1997 was the best year for Justin when he won the Kemper Open and his first major tournament, the British Open, and two million dollars for the year. The story of his winning the British Open is an interesting one: one that shows the intensity and determination of Justin Leonard.

Justin had made serious preparations for winning the British Open some day. In 1996, he was not exempt from qualifying for the tournament. So without knowing whether or not he could make the field he went over to England on his own. He did qualify successfully and went on to experience British golf for the first time.The scene was Royal Lytham at Lytham St. Anne's, England on the western shore of England near the famous seaside resort of Blackpool.

Lytham St. Anne's is a links-type of golf course, built on seaside sand and surrounded by gorse, a spiny evergreen shrub which grows to a height of four or five feet and affords the golfer a most unpleasant experience when he happens to find his golf ball lying in or under one of these bushes. Here he learned to dig the ball successfully out of the long foot high, sometimes two foot high rough. Since Justin is a low-ball hitter he realized his game was eminently suited to conquer the strong winds which blew in off the sea. Leonard finished well down the list but he gained valuable experience in seaside golf. Fast forward to 1997. Justin entered the 1997 British Open at the Famous Royal Troon Golf Club in Troon, Scotland intending to win and capitalize on his earlier experience at Lytham St. Anne's.

On the first day of play Leonard opened with a 69 under blustery conditions, never hitting a green in regulation. His second round was a smooth 66 for 135. In the meantime Darren Clarke, the Irishman, was even better off with 67-66-133 and Jesper Parnevik was in with 70-66-136.

Clarke eventually fell off the pace with closing 71s. By the last day, Parnevik was in front with a third round of 66-202. He was five strokes ahead of Leonard who had posted a third round of 72.

On the last day, Leonard simply out-played Parnevik and Clarke. Five strokes behind at the start, he caught Jesper when he holed a 30-foot putt on the seventeenth green as Jesper, playing behind him missed a birdie putt at sixteen from five feet. Jesper faded at the last hole and finished three strokes behind Leonard, tied with Darren Clarke for second place.

At the age of 25, Justin Leonard was the youngest winner of the British Open since Seve Ballesteros won the 1979 British Open at the age of 22.

Here are the final scores of the 1997 British Open:

Justin Leonard	69-66-72-65—272	$418,875
Darren Clarke	67-66-71-71—275	$251,325
Jesper Parnevik	70-66-66-73—275	$251,325
Jim Furyk	67-72-70-70—279	$150,795

Will Justin Leonard be another Ben Hogan? Time alone will tell. He won his first major championship before Hogan did.

INDEX